FOOD AND SHELTER

A Drama in Two Acts

by Jane Anderson

SAMUEL FRENCH, INC.

45 WEST 25TH STREET   NEW YORK 10010
7623 SUNSET BOULEVARD   HOLLYWOOD 90046
LONDON   *TORONTO*

Copyright © 1992 by Jane Anderson

IMPORTANT BILLING AND CREDIT
REQUIREMENTS

All producers of FOOD AND SHELTER *must* give credit to the Author of the Play in all programs distributed in connection with performances of the Play and in all instances in which the title of the Play appears for purposes of advertising, publicizing or otherwise exploiting the Play and/or a production. The name of the Author *must* also appear on a separate line, on which no other name appears, immediately following the title, and *must* appear in size of type not less than fifty percent the size of the title type.

ACKNOWLEDGEMENTS

In addition to the aforementioned people who were tremendously helpful in the development of *Food and Shelter*, the playwright wishes to acknowledge the following for their help and support: Tess Ayers, Martin Gage, The Los Angeles Writer's Bloc, Susan Merson and Tony Schultz, and The Raphael House.

Food And Shelter was produced by the American Conservatory Theater in December 1990. It was directed by Joy Carlin and had the following cast:

EARL...Ed Hodson
LOIS ....Cathy Thomas-Grant
CHRISSIE...Alden Fletcher
....Jennifer Lorch
LAMAR..Michael McFall
DISNEYLAND COP......................... Richard Butterfield
.... James Patrick Kennedy
LIBRARIAN.......................................Judith Moreland
CLERK... Tim Lord

Scenery & Costumes: Gerard Howland
Lighting: Derek Duarte
Music & Sound: Stephen LeGrand
Production Stage Manager: Alice Elliott

The play was subsequently produced at The Vineyard Theatre, New York City, May 1991. It was directed by Andre Ernotte and had the following cast:

LOIS ....Kelly Coffield
EARL...................................Philip Seymour Hoffman
CHRISSIE...T-F Walker
LAMAR...Isiah Whitlock Jr.
COP/CLERK.....................................John Speredakos
LIBRARIAN..Virginia Wing

Scenery: Ann Sheffield
Costumes: Muriel Stockdale
Lighting: Donald Holder
Sound & Music: Aural Fixation
Production Stage Manager: Crystal Huntington

CHARACTERS

LOIS—in her mid to late twenties. From the East Coast.

EARL—her husband. In his mid to late twenties, also from the East Coast.

CHRISSIE—their four-year-old daughter (can be played by an older child who looks young.)

LAMAR—a black man in his twenties to early thirties.

A DISNEYLAND COP/ A CLERK: both these parts can be played by one actor—someone who would match Earl's age.

A LIBRARIAN—a woman in her forties, not necessarily white, and not necessarily American-born.

TIME

Present day

PLACE

Act I takes place in Disneyland.

Act II is one week to three months later and takes place in various locations around Hollywood and East Los Angeles.

N.B. [/]: means the next speech begins here.

THE SETTINGS

The locations do not have to be taken literally. The Act I set does not have to be a blow-by-blow recreation of Disneyland. You couldn't do that anyway, because Disney would probably come around and wave a lawsuit in your face. Everything can be a suggestion—shadows of birds for the Enchanted Tiki Room, a ladder disappearing into a wash of leaves for the Swiss Family Robinson House. Let the lights, the sound, the actors, and especially the audience fill everything else in. There should be no pauses between scenes. The only scenic piece should be some representation of the Matterhorn looming up behind like a big, dumb, friendly presence that reflects the artificial magic of the place.

Act II should also be kept simple. The transitions between scenes should be as immediate as a sound and light cue. If we have to wait for set changes or for a car to be hauled on and off the stage, the play will die a slow death. I'd be happy if the car was simply two chairs pushed together and lit by a special to indicate a street light shining intrusively through the windshield.

The simplicity of the production should be stylish, almost Japanese. Lights and shadows play a big part in this play. Please don't take the subject of poverty too literally—go easy on the graffiti and chain link fencing. Leave room in the design for the possibility of angels.

AUTHOR'S NOTE

If I could wish anything for a production of this play, I would wish that it be funny, romantic and magical—which are not things that you would normally associate with homelessness. Please, if anything, play against the darkness. This is not a political tract on poverty in America. I've written a play about a regular family in a bad situation who are doing what they can to keep themselves together. It's a folk fable.

On the matter of Chrissie and the angel... I don't think it matters whether you believe in angels or not (although, personally, I do.) Children can make magic—whether it's real or imaginary. And when children sense that the world around them is out of control, they call on their own special powers to conjure up a personal protector. The Archangel Raphael is the angel of family and home. His name means: "God has healed."

Jane Anderson
Los Angeles, California
October, 1991

ACT I

Scene 1

*The New Orleans section of Disneyland. EARL and LOIS
are sitting on a bench with their four-year-old, Chrissie.
THEY're exhausted. CHRISSIE is whining.*

EARL. Chrissie, come on, stop whining.
CHRISSIE. I want a cookie.
EARL. They don't have cookies here.
LOIS. We can get you an ice cream, would you like
that?
CHRISSIE. Nooo.
LOIS. O.K., maybe Daddy will find you a cookie
somewhere.
EARL. She doesn't need a cookie.

(CHRISSIE whines.)

EARL. Chrissie, I don't want to hear it.
LOIS. She should have one.
EARL. Not when she starts whining for everything she
wants.
LOIS. Earl, this is Disneyland. She's supposed to get
everything she wants.
EARL. She's gotten everything she wanted for the past
four hours and look how unhappy she is.
CHRISSIE. I want a *cookie*!

EARL. Hey! You want to go to the car?
CHRISSIE. No.
EARL. Then be happy.
LOIS. She has a craving.
EARL. What's to crave? Jesus, I took her on all her favorite rides twice. She met Snow White. The man let her touch the bird in the Tiki Room. She's had a perfect day. Chrissie, didn't you have fun today?

(CHRISSIE shakes her head no.)

EARL. Do you know how much it cost Daddy to bring us here?
LOIS. Earl, lay off her.
EARL. Jesus, Chrissie. This was supposed to be your special treat.

(CHRISSIE starts to cry.)

LOIS. Now you made her cry. What's the matter with you?
EARL. This was supposed to be a good day for her. I don't know what the problem is.
LOIS. Chrissie, come here, sit with Mommy. You want to take a nap?

(CHRISSIE curls up on Lois' lap.)

EARL. Forgive me for assuming she was having a nice day.
LOIS. Maybe it was a long day for her and she got a little cranky at the end. Did you think of that?

EARL. Maybe I'm cranky too. I get cranky too, Lois.
LOIS. So do I, but I try not to take it out on Chrissie.
EARL. I'm sorry.

(LOIS doesn't say anything.)

EARL. I said I'm sorry.
LOIS. O.K., Earl.
EARL. Chrissie, you forgive me? You forgive Daddy
for being an asshole?
LOIS. Don't use that word around her.
EARL. Chrissie, you forgive Daddy for being stupid
and for using bad language in front of you?

*(CHRISSIE shakes her head and buries her face in Lois'
   arm.)*

EARL. Come on, Chrissie, even if I say I'm really,
really sorry?

(CHRISSIE shakes her head.)

EARL. Even if Daddy promises to get you a cookie?
You gonna be my friend again? (EARL starts to tickle
Chrissie.)*

(SHE giggles.)

EARL. Come over and sit with Daddy. I have to know
if you're still my friend.

(CHRISSIE crawls over onto Earl's lap.)

EARL. Maybe later I'll take you on the Teacups. I'll show you how to make them spin.

LOIS. Ooh, you'd like the Teacups, Chrissie.

EARL. You'd like to do that?

CHRISSIE. Yeah.

EARL. O.K., then.

(A beat.)

LOIS. How much did we save for dinner?

EARL. Lemme check.

LOIS. I saw they have a chicken dinner with vegetables and mashed potatoes in the restaurant over there. It's cafeteria-style so we wouldn't have to worry about a tip.

EARL. How much is it, the dinner?

LOIS. Eight dollars.

EARL. Jesus, I didn't think the food would be so expensive here.

CHRISSIE. I want some vegetables.

LOIS. We'll get some for you, Chrissie.

EARL. We're gonna cut into the gas money.

LOIS. They got salads I think, for about three fifty.

EARL. That's not a dinner.

LOIS. They got cheese and ham in the salad. It looked very nutritious.

EARL. It's not gonna be enough.

LOIS. You think we should we try to make it back for the food kitchen?

EARL. We'd have to leave now.

LOIS. We'll miss the fireworks. Maybe we could go and then come back?

EARL. It's a two hour drive. We'd use up all our gas.

LOIS. You think they have any food kitchens around here?

EARL. Orange county is for theme parks. Where are they gonna put a soup kitchen?

LOIS. I wanted Chrissie to see the fireworks.

EARL. Yeah, well I want to see the fireworks too.

LOIS. You know what we should do? We'll get a salad and ask for some bread. Then later we can have some popcorn. Popcorn is very filling.

EARL. Popcorn makes you thirsty, then you gotta buy a drink.

LOIS. They got water here. They'll let you drink free from the water for God's sake.

EARL. Yeah, O.K.

CHRISSIE. Do I get a cookie?

LOIS. Honey, you're gonna get some popcorn instead.

CHRISSIE. No...

LOIS. Honey, you like popcorn. Remember how you liked Jiffy Pop? Remember how that was a special treat?

CHRISSIE. Yeah.

LOIS. And when it gets dark the Magic Castle will light up and then we'll see the fireworks.

CHRISSIE. I want to see the pirates again.

EARL. Chrissie, no. The line's too long.

LOIS. Honey, why don't you lay down in my lap and take a nap? Earl, let me lean against you while Chrissie and I take a little nap.

(LOIS leans against Earl.))

LOIS. Maybe you should put your arm around me so it doesn't look like I'm sleeping. Do we look O.K.?

EARL. No one's noticing.

LOIS. People notice. People notice when someone looks bummy.

EARL. We don't look bummy. We just look like we've been on too many rides.

EARL. Where do you wanna park the car tonight?

LOIS. Maybe we can spend the night in the lot. Don't they have that part where the campers park?

EARL. I think they got guards walking around.

LOIS. It'd be nice if Chrissie could wake up and see the Matterhorn.

EARL. Yeah, I'll check it out. (*A beat.*) That chicken dinner sounds good. Maybe if we say we'll take all wings, they'll give us a discount.

CHRISSIE. I want a cookie.

LOIS. Honey, shhhh.

CHRISSIE. (*Restless.*) Mommy?

LOIS. What, honey?

CHRISSIE. Can we go on the pirate ride?

EARL. The line's too long.

CHRISSIE. Please?

EARL. I don't want to stand in any more lines right now.

CHRISSIE. Mommeee...

LOIS. Honey, don't whine.

EARL. (*To Lois.*) We have any cigarettes left?

LOIS. No.

CHRISSIE. (*Starts to squirm.*) I want to do something.

LOIS. Earl, take her on something without a line.

EARL. You want to do Tom Sawyer's Island?

(CHRISSIE shrugs.)

EARL. It's up to you, Chrissie. *(Starts looking for something on the ground.)*
LOIS. *(To Chrissie.)* Go do the island with your daddy. Then when you come back we're gonna have something to eat.
CHRISSIE. I'm hungry.
LOIS. I know. And then after we eat we'll go over in front of the castle and watch the fireworks and Tinkerbell will be flying down.
CHRISSIE. I wanna do the pirates instead.
LOIS. Oh, but Chrissie, the fireworks are gonna be something beautiful to remember. Don't you want beautiful things to remember?
CHRISSIE. Yes.
LOIS. Well, this will be one of them. *(Noticing Earl hunting around.)* Earl, what are you doing?
EARL. Looking for a cigarette.
LOIS. Jesus, when did you start doing that?
EARL. I wouldn't do it on a regular street. It's very sanitary here.
LOIS. For God's sake, you want them to kick us out?
EARL. They aren't gonna kick us out.
LOIS. What kind of bummy behavior is that, looking for butts.
EARL. It isn't bummy if it's clean. It's like picking a piece of fruit off the tree. You pick it up, you wipe it off.
LOIS. I don't know what you're gonna find. Everything gets swept up.
EARL. Yeah, I know.

LOIS. I don't want you to start doing that. It's dirty. I'm not gonna kiss you anymore.

EARL. So? We haven't been kissing anyway.

LOIS. Chrissie, go with Daddy. Go play on the island.

EARL. Come on, Chrissie.

LOIS. (*To Earl.*) I'll stay here. I might go freshen up in the rest room, maybe brush my teeth. Then we'll eat, O.K.?

EARL. Yeah, O.K.

(EARL and CHRISSIE leave.

LOIS stays on the bench. We hear the SOUNDS OF FAMILIES as they walk by. LOIS is watching them, very self-conscious. SHE pulls their belongings closer. SHE discreetly checks to see if she has B.O. WE hear a PARADE coming towards us—very goofy Disneyland MUSIC. LOIS, sees it and follows it with her eyes. The utter silliness of it makes her laugh and for a minute, SHE's taken out of herself.)

FADE OUT

Scene 2

EARL is returning to the bench, carrying CHRISSIE on his shoulders.

EARL. ...Tom Sawyer was this kid who went down the river on a raft with his buddy Huck. One day they just took off. Decided they had enough, just got the hell out of there.

LOIS. (*To Chrissie.*) Did you have a good time?
CHRISSIE. Yeah.
LOIS. What did you do?
CHRISSIE. We did jumping things.
LOIS. Uh-huh.
CHRISSIE. And we climbed and we crossed bridges.
LOIS. Oh boy, you did a lot. I bet you're hungry.
CHRISSIE. Yes.
LOIS. (*Pulls out a hot dog with a bite taken out of it.*) Look what I have.
EARL. You bought food already?
LOIS. I didn't buy it. I met a woman and we started talking and she bought us a hot dog.

(CHRISSIE starts wolfing down the hot dog.)

EARL. Chrissie, go easy. Try to eat it slow. (*To Lois.*) So who was this woman?
LOIS. A divorcee. She was waiting for her boys who were on the pirate ride and we got to talking. Oh, she had some terrible stories about her husband. She supported him through medical school, right? But then he was sued for malpractice and he had to quit the profession. And then one day she comes home from marketing, she finds him doing it with her best friend in the swimming pool. Not only that, he was a gambler and got them into terrible debt. They lost their house, it was only a year ago.
EARL. Uh-huh.
LOIS. So she filed for a divorce, and moved to Pomona. Now she raises Lhasa Apsos and she's doing very well.
EARL. Huh.
LOIS. So people can rise above their circumstances.

EARL. Yeah, but she had money.

LOIS. I told you, her husband lost it all.

EARL. Yeah, but she probably had something left in an account. She started a business, right?

LOIS. Well regardless, I thought it was an interesting story. (*A beat.*) So you were gone a long time. Did you have fun?

EARL. Yeah. I had an interesting conversation with someone.

(*A beat.*)

LOIS. Well good, you wanna talk about it?

EARL. You wanna spend the night here instead of going back to the car?

LOIS. What are you saying?

EARL. It's very simple. We go on Tom Sawyer's Island while everyone goes to the fireworks. They got places to hide on the island. They'd never find us.

LOIS. Of course they would.

EARL. No one goes on Tom Sawyer's Island. It's a stupid attraction. Who would be on Tom Sawyer's Island during the fireworks? They wouldn't even bother to check.

LOIS. Of course they check. They probably have infrared things and detectors. And anyway you have to get on that mechanical raft to go to the Island. How we gonna get on and off without them knowing?

EARL. We'll borrow a canoe.

LOIS. The canoes are attached to an underwater thing.

EARL. I checked it out when I was down there with Chrissie. I talked to a guy who works here. He showed me how you unhook them.

LOIS. Oh smart, you talked to one of them about it? How do you know he won't report us?

EARL. He won't report us. He offered me a joint.

LOIS. You didn't smoke with him, did you?

EARL. No, I'm just telling you what kind of guy he was. He got the job 'cause his uncle services Space Mountain.

LOIS. (*Takes this in.*) So we can paddle out there in a canoe? You know how to do a canoe without it tipping over?

EARL. Sure I know how to do a canoe. What I'll do, I'll go to the car, bring us back some blankets, maybe a change of clothes. Then we can have a leisurely something to eat, then we go out there, watch the fire works. Then when everyone's gone, maybe we'll take a little ride in the canoe, look at the stars. Then I could drop you and Chrissie off at those rest rooms you liked in Bear Country.

LOIS. What if they catch us?

EARL. What are they gonna do? So they tell us to leave. So what?

LOIS. They won't arrest us or anything?

EARL. They wouldn't arrest the homeless. It would be bad press.

LOIS. Chrissie, would you like that? You want to spend the night in Disneyland instead of the car?

CHRISSIE. Yeah!

LOIS. (*To Earl.*) Can we still see the fireworks from the island?

EARL. Sure.

LOIS. We can do this?

EARL. I told you.

LOIS. It would be like a real vacation, wouldn't it?

EARL. Like camping, yeah.
LOIS. Jesus, Earl, I don't know.
EARL. Why not?
LOIS. We might as well, right? It could be very good for us.
EARL. That's why I'm suggesting it.
LOIS. ...instead of going back to the car.
EARL. Sure.
LOIS. I think we should. Let's stay. We've earned it, Earl.

FADE OUT

Scene 3

A restaurant in the New Orleans section. LOIS and CHRISSIE are sharing a salad. There are several condiments on the table, along with a few rolls.
LOIS is squeezing lemon wedges into a glass of water.

LOIS. (*To Chrissie.*) You want to help Mommy make some lemonade? Take a piece of lemon, squeeze it in to the cup, that right's...

(EARL enters with a roll of blankets.)

LOIS. (*To Earl.*) Everything go alright?
EARL. This Nazi guy at the gate wanted to know what I was doing with the blankets. I told him I needed them for

my wife who was in a wheel chair so she wouldn't get cold during the fireworks.

LOIS. Good. What'd he say?

EARL. He wanted to know if we were satisfied with the handicap facilities and if we had any problems to let him know. (*EARL pours ketchup on a roll and eats.*)

LOIS. I took Chrissie on the Tea Cups while you were gone.

EARL. Yeah, was it fun?

LOIS. Well I finally figured out how to make the tea cup spin.

EARL. Uh-huh.

LOIS. And I got it spinning like crazy and I held on to Chrissie and I leaned my head back—you know how when you're on a wild ride it's O.K. to scream?

EARL. Yeah.

LOIS. Well I screamed at the top of my lungs the entire time and I'm telling you, Earl, it felt so good.

EARL. Yeah?

LOIS. Maybe I'll take you on it later on. It's like a release.

EARL. Chrissie was it good for you?

CHRISSIE. It was *scary.* And then, Daddy, you know what we did? We went to the Snow White wishing well.

EARL. Oh Yeah?

CHRISSIE. Mommy found a shiny gum wrapper and made it into a nickel.

(*LOIS is mixing some sugar in with the lemon water.*)

EARL. (*To Chrissie.*) Yeah, so did you throw it in and make a wish?

CHRISSIE. Uh-huh. And then one of the Dwarfs came over. He scared me.
EARL. He did?
CHRISSIE. His face was too big.
LOIS. (*Handing Chrissie the lemon water.*) Here's your lemonade, honey. Drink it. It has vitamin C.

(CHRISSIE tastes it and makes a face.)

LOIS. Too sour? Here, I'll put a little more sugar.
EARL. So, what'd you wish for, Chrissie?
CHRISSIE. Something to eat.
LOIS. (*Handing Chrissie the lemon water.*) Here, honey, try this now.

(CHRISSIE tastes it. It's fine. SHE starts drinking it down in great gulps.)

EARL. Chrissie, slow down.
LOIS. (*Takes the glass from Chrissie.*) We'll take a little rest, O.K.?
EARL. Do they have any of those cream containers? Maybe we could put together a glass of milk for her.
LOIS. I checked. It's non-dairy.
EARL. Jesus, what's wrong with this place? Everything's either processed or it costs. America's fucked.
LOIS. Earl, come on. This is our special night.
LOIS. (*Makes a sandwich for herself.*) It's kinda nice to know that everyone here is gonna have to get in their cars and leave but we can just sit here and relax.

EARL. (*Staring at a table across from them.*) Those people left a plate of french fries over there. They didn't even touch them.

LOIS. I don't want to take from other people's plates.

EARL. They're just gonna get thrown out.

LOIS. I don't want to be scavenging on our special night.

EARL. We're not gonna enjoy ourselves if we're walking around with empty stomachs. We'll have a lousy time 'cause we won't be thinking of anything else.

(A beat.)

LOIS. Go ahead.

(The LIGHTS CROSS FADE as EARL gets up and walks into a spot with a MAN in a straw hat and old-fashioned sleeve garters. He's one of those undercover Disneyland cops who is required to walk around in a theme costume.)

COP. Have you looked for work?

EARL. Of course I have.

COP. And?

EARL. I couldn't find anything.

COP. I open the paper every day, I see all kinds of jobs.

EARL. Hey, you think I was sitting on my butt waiting for the rent to run out? If you want I'll write down for you every bill we had to pay while / I was running around looking for work....

COP. Hey, I've been working since I was sixteen years old ...

EARL. So have I. Jesus, we aren't lazy people...

COP. ...just the other day I saw a sign in a Carl Jr.'s. / My gosh, you have your health, you're an able-bodied guy...

EARL. (*Over him.*) ...I was shoveling snow for neighbors just so we could pay for stupid things like toothpaste.

COP. I understand, Mr. Randazzo, but Disneyland is not the place to vent your frustrations.

EARL. My child was hungry.

COP. Have you applied for food stamps?

EARL. We use them.

COP. Then I don't understand the problem, do you?

EARL. Let me tell you something about food stamps, O.K.? My wife and me, we went to a market and we wanted to buy one of those cooked chickens they got in the deli section for our dinner. But you can't get cooked food with food stamps. You can get potato chips and bean dip and all kinds of packaged crap, but real food you can only get raw. Which is crazy because a lot of people in our position, we don't have stoves. And I'm trying to reason as well as I can with the manager, he can see in front of him that Chrissie is thin and has circles under her eyes and should be eating something better than baloney and white bread. You know what I would have done if I was this manager? I'd say, "Hey, go ahead. Take the chicken. God Bless." Isn't that what you do when you see someone in need?

COP. Where is this going, Mr. Randazzo?

EARL. I took the five dollars the chicken would of cost and I bought some lottery tickets. My wife yelled at me, said it was a stupid thing to do.

COP. I agree.

EARL. Hey. I won a hundred dollars.

COP. Congratulations. That still doesn't answer my question.

EARL. I'm telling you. So my wife and me, we decided to take Chrissie to Disneyland.

COP. Instead of providing her with a decent meal. That's what I would have done.

EARL. We got her a decent meal. Jesus. The night before we came here we went to, what do you call it, the Sizzler. She had a hamburger and shrimp. We took her through the salad bar twice. She ate so much she threw it all up. It didn't even take. And then you gotta ask, how many meals like that are you gonna get with a hundred dollars? But Disneyland. This is something to feed her soul.

(As we FADE OUT on this scene, we hear the pop and whistle of FIREWORKS exploding overhead.
LIGHTS UP on LOIS and CHRISSIE in a canoe at the edge of the Frontierland lagoon. LOIS is holding Chrissie, who's bundled up in some blankets. EARL joins them.)

LOIS. Aren't they pretty Chrissie?

(They're in the DARK for a moment. We hear a WHISTLE.)

LOIS. Ooh, what's this one gonna be? (*A beat.*) No, it looks like that one might be a dud.

(We hear a series of EXPLOSIONS, the sky LIGHTS up.)

LOIS. Oh my God, oh Chrissie, look at that. It looks like a bunch of angels are having a party up there, doesn't it?

(More EXPLOSIONS. It grows BRIGHTER. This is the finale. One final REPORT, then the LIGHT in the sky begins to fade.)

EARL. What did you think of that, Chrissie?
CHRISSIE. *(Quietly.)* That's the most beautiful thing I've seen in my entire life.

(A beat. THEY wait to see if there are any more. Then EARL begins to paddle.)

EARL. You wanna go see the Indians, Chrissie?
CHRISSIE. Nooo!
LOIS. Earl, she doesn't want to. They scared her before.
EARL. They aren't real, Chrissie. They're robots. Daddy will show you they're fake.
CHRISSIE. Nooo!
LOIS. We don't need to see the Indians.
EARL. Maybe we should go over to Jungle Land, look at the hippos.
CHRISSIE. Yeah!
LOIS. Honey, I thought you were afraid of the hippos.
CHRISSIE. No, they're cute.
EARL. We'll paddle down near Bear Country, I think there's a part there that connects.

LOIS. No it doesn't. This is a different body of water from Jungle Land.

EARL. Let me just try it.

LOIS. Fine. Go ahead.

EARL. Once in a while I've been right.

LOIS. Did you hear me? I said go ahead.

LOIS. Just don't tip us over.

EARL. I'm not gonna tip us over.

LOIS. *(Adjusting Chrissie's blanket.)* Chrissie, are you warm enough?

CHRISSIE. Yeah.

LOIS. Are you having fun?

CHRISSIE. Yeah.

LOIS. Oh Chrissie, look. There's the Matterhorn. They left it lighted for us. Isn't that pretty? Earl, look.

EARL. Yeah, it's truly magnificent.

LOIS. This was a wonderful idea that you had.

EARL. Thank you, Lois. *(EARL stops paddling.)*

(THEY're quiet for a beat, enjoying the night. We hear a FROG croak.)

LOIS. Is that a frog?

EARL. Yeah.

LOIS. You think it's real?

EARL. They got everything turned off so it must be.

LOIS. I wonder if they brought the frog here or if the frog came here on its own?

EARL. I'm sure they brought it in.

LOIS. Well, maybe the frog got washed into the area through a drainage pipe or something and then its instincts led him to Disneyland. Animals can do that. They have extra senses that guide them to where it's habitable for them to live.

EARL. Disneyland is surrounded by five miles of parking lot, Lois, the frog would of been hit by a car.

LOIS. Well maybe the frog hopped over here at night. Or maybe his instincts led him around the tires of the cars.

CHRISSIE. Can we visit the frog?

EARL. Okie dokie, Chrissie. (*HE starts paddling again.*)

LOIS. Animals can do that. No matter what happens, they always manage to find a place to live.

EARL. Sometimes they don't. A lot of animals, you fuck with their habitat, they get wiped out.

LOIS. Not all of them. Some survive.

CHRISSIE. I want to touch the frog.

(*The FROG stops croaking.*)

CHRISSIE. Where's the frog?

(*EARL and LOIS listen.*)

EARL. It's hiding, Chrissie. It doesn't want you to touch it.

FADE OUT

Scene 4

The Women's Rest Room in the Bear Country section of Disneyland. LOIS is giving CHRISSIE a wash down at the sink.

LOIS. Does that feel good Chrissie?

CHRISSIE. The water's cold.

LOIS. O.K., we'll make it a little warmer for you. (*SHE adjusts the water.*) That better?

CHRISSIE. Yeah.

LOIS. (*Gently dries Chrissie's back with a a paper towel.*) Is that too rough?

CHRISSIE. No.

LOIS. Here, we'll keep your sweater on the parts we already dried. You warmer now?

CHRISSIE. Yes.

LOIS. (*Works on the back of Chrissie's neck.*) Ooh, you got a lot of dirt back here. What, are you trying to start a garden?

(CHRISSIE giggles.)

LOIS. I see a carrot back here. You didn't tell me you were growing carrots.

(CHRISSIE giggles.
EARL enters. HE leans against one of the sinks.)

LOIS. Earl, you aren't supposed to be in here. This is the Ladies Room.

EARL. So arrest me.

LOIS. (*To Chrissie.*) Ooh, Daddy's in the Ladies Room.

CHRISSIE. Daddy, this room is only for *ladies*.

EARL. Yeah? So then what are the two of you doing in here?

LOIS. Ooh, Daddy's being smart with us, Chrissie.

CHRISSIE. Daddy's a real smartie pants.

LOIS. (*To Earl.*) So did you wash already?

EARL. Yeah.

LOIS. Come over here, let me take a look.

LOIS. (*Inspects the back of Earl's neck.*) You did a very good job.

EARL. Thank you.

LOIS. Is that after-shave I smell?

EARL. Yeah. I had some left in the car.

LOIS. (*Nuzzles Earl's neck.*) Ooh, you smell good.

EARL. (*Nuzzles Lois' neck.*) You smell pretty good too. (*To Chrissie.*) What about you? Do you smell good? (*EARL nuzzles Chrissie's neck.*)

(*SHE giggles.*)

EARL. Yeah, Chrissie smells good too.

LOIS. She does? Let me see. (*Nuzzles Chrissie's neck.*) Yes she does. She smells just like a flower.

EARL. All of us are smelling good tonight.

LOIS. I washed my hair. I dried it under the hand blower.

EARL. Lemme see. (*EARL nuzzles Lois again. HE's starting to feel sexy.*) Yeah, your hair smells nice.

LOIS. Let me finish with Chrissie.

EARL. I thought maybe when you're done, I'd take both of you out for a stroll up Main Street.

LOIS. That would be nice.

EARL. Then we'll put Chrissie to bed and we'll take another walk somewhere...

LOIS. Maybe we can do that.

CHRISSIE. Can I sleep with the Tiki birds?

EARL. Sure. If we can get in there.

CHRISSIE. I want them to sing to me.

LOIS. It won't be running right now, but you can pretend.

EARL. (*Puts his arms around Lois.*) You're a beautiful woman.

LOIS. Thank you, Earl.

(*LIGHTS CROSS FADE to Cop.*)

COP. I can't tell you how appalled we are by this.

EARL. Look, I don't know if you're married or not, are you married? You have a girlfriend?

(*A beat. The COP is caught off guard.*)

EARL. Hey, don't tell me you never thought about doing what I did.

(*The COP and EARL laugh briefly.*)

COP. That's not what we're talking about right now.

EARL. It is. Yes it is. I'm talking about still wanting to be with your wife in an intimate way. It's a hard thing to do when you haven't had privacy in six months.

COP. You caused hundreds of dollars worth of damage, Mr. Randazzo. You can't go around destroying private property to take care of your personal needs.

EARL. Jesus, that's not what we set out to do.

COP. Whatever you were doing, that's not what the park was / designed for.

EARL. For the first time in months, my wife looked beautiful to me. Can't you understand that?

COP. Whatever you want to do with your wife should be conducted in the privacy of your own bedroom.

EARL. We don't *have* a bedroom.

COP. That's not our problem.

(A beat.)

COP. ...how was the mattress?
EARL. It was full of newspaper.
COP. Shit.

(The COP and EARL laugh again.)

FADE OUT

Scene 5

The Enchanted Tiki Room. LOIS is bundling CHRISSIE up in some blankets, trying to make a makeshift bed.

LOIS. Can you feel the floor? Is it still too hard for you?

CHRISSIE. Put feathers under me.

LOIS. We don't have any feathers, Chrissie.

CHRISSIE. Take the feathers from the Tiki birds.

LOIS. We can't do that.

CHRISSIE. Why not?

LOIS. It's destruction of property.

CHRISSIE. Oh.

LOIS. Honey, I'm gonna take a little walk with Daddy. Then we'll be right back. I want you to close your eyes and get some sleep.

CHRISSIE. I don't want to sleep here.

LOIS. I thought you said you wanted to be with the Tiki Birds.

CHRISSIE. They might make doodie on me.

LOIS. Chrissie, they won't.

CHRISSIE. Why not?

LOIS. They aren't alive. Therefore, they don't make doodie.

CHRISSIE. Oh.

LOIS. Do you want to sleep somewhere else?

CHRISSIE. No.

LOIS. We're gonna be right outside. I'll be back in a little bit and then I'll take a nap with you. O.K?

CHRISSIE. I'm not sleepy.

LOIS. Why don't you close your eyes and pretend that all the birds are watching over you and singing you their song. Can you do that?

CHRISSIE. Uh-huh.

LOIS. They're gonna make sure nothing bad happens while I'm gone. Can you think about that?

CHRISSIE. O.K. (*A beat.*) Mommy? Does Tinkerbell come from God?

LOIS. No, Chrissie.

CHRISSIE. I thought she did.

LOIS. Tinkerbell's a fairy. Only angels come from God.

CHRISSIE. Oh.

LOIS. But you can believe in Tinkerbell if you want.

CHRISSIE. If I believe in Tinkerbell, do I have to believe in Jesus?

LOIS. Well, you can believe whatever you want. But it's easier to believe in Jesus. You don't find a lot of churches devoted to Tinkerbell.

CHRISSIE. I don't like Jesus.

LOIS. Why?

CHRISSIE. Because they talked about him at the mission.

LOIS. Yeah, I know.

CHRISSIE. There was doodie on the bathroom floor.

LOIS. I know. It wasn't a very nice place.

CHRISSIE. Jesus did it.

LOIS. No he didn't, honey. Jesus wouldn't do that.

CHRISSIE. Well, I don't want him around.

LOIS. O.K., you don't have to have him around if you don't want to.

CHRISSIE. Does Captain Eo come from God?

LOIS. No honey, Captain Eo comes from Michael Jackson.

CHRISSIE. But I believe in him.

LOIS. Honey, whatever will get you through the day. O.K., go to sleep.

CHRISSIE. Captain Eo is everywhere.

LOIS. I know. Good night.

FADE OUT

Scene 6

EARL is leading LOIS to the bottom of the Swiss Family Robinson Treehouse.

LOIS. Earl, why can't you kiss me down here on the ground?

EARL. 'Cause it's better up in a tree.

LOIS. I don't want to leave Chrissie alone too long.

EARL. She's sleeping.

LOIS. What do you wanna go in the tree for?

EARL. The view's better. And I wanna do more than just kiss you.

LOIS. Yeah? Like what?

EARL. They got a bed up there.

LOIS. You wanna seduce me in the Swiss Family Robinson bed?

EARL. Uh-huh.

LOIS. Oh Early, I don't think they designed it for that.

EARL. Why not?

LOIS. It's supposed to be a family attraction.

EARL. So? We're family.

LOIS. Little kids will be going up there tomorrow.

EARL. Chrissie used to walk through our bedroom in the morning, she never knew. We're husband and wife. What's wrong with making love in the privacy of our own tree?

(EARL takes LOIS' hand and leads her up the ladder to the tree.)

LOIS. Earl, we got to be careful. I don't have any protection.

EARL. I'll be careful.

LOIS. You remember the days when we had a house and it was still sexy to do it in the car?

EARL. Yeah. Let's not think about that right now.

(THEY climb into the tree house.)

FADE OUT

Scene 7

The Tiki Bird House. CHRISSIE is lying on her back, pretending that her rag doll is talking to one of the Tiki Birds.

CHRISSIE. *(As the doll.)* Hello, Mr. Bird. I need somewhere to sleep. Can I come visit your house? *(As the bird.)* How are you going to get up here? *(As the doll.)* Why don't you put me on your back and fly me up there? *(As the bird.)* I'm busy cleaning my feathers. Go ask someone else. *(As the doll.)* OK. *(To another bird.)* Hello, Mr. Bird. Will you fly me up to your house? *(As the bird.)* I can't. My wing is broken. Go ask someone else. *(As the doll, to another bird.)* OK. Hello, Mr. Bird. Will you fly me up to your house? *(As the bird.)* Why don't I sprinkle magic dust on you and you can do it yourself? *(As the *doll.*) OK. (*CHRISSIE makes magic whooshing noises. As the bird.*) There. All set. Come on up.

(*CHRISSIE holds her doll up. SHE releases it and it flies up.*)

BLACKOUT

Scene 8

EARL is sitting on the top of the stairs of the tree house, smoking a cigarette. LOIS is still up in the tree.

EARL. Lois, come on.
LOIS. Don't you think we should try to fix it?
EARL. We don't have nothing to fix it with. Don't worry about it.
LOIS. (*Appears at the top of the stairs. SHE is giggling.*) Oh, Jesus, the whole thing is collapsed. All these people are gonna be walking by tomorrow, they're gonna be wondering what the Swiss Robinsons were up to.
EARL. It's realism, Lois. Come and sit with me.
LOIS. We should get back to Chrissie soon.
EARL. I know.
LOIS. So where did this cigarette come from?

(*EARL shrugs.*)

LOIS. Great, I'm glad I kissed you already.

EARL. My lips aren't even touching it. See? (*EARL holds the cigarette so he inhales the smoke through his fingers.*) You want a puff?

(*EARL holds the cigarette for Lois while SHE takes a puff.*)

LOIS. Ooh, it's mentholated. Good choice, Earl.
EARL. C'mere, baby.
LOIS. You love me Early?
EARL. With all my heart plus more.
LOIS. I want us to always make love 'cause we want to, not 'cause we're too depressed to do anything else.
EARL. It's a deal.
LOIS. I'm still worried about the bed. Maybe I should put a grass mat over it or something.
EARL. Don't worry about it. They got to fix things here all the time.
LOIS. Don't you feel a little bit like Adam and Eve messing up in Paradise?
EARL. This isn't Paradise.
LOIS. A little bit. The trees are nice.
EARL. Half of them are made of cement. If this were Paradise, the trees would have fruit and we'd be picking something for Chrissie to eat.
LOIS. Didn't Orange County use to be an orchard?
EARL. I don't know.

(*The LIGHT is starting to change. We hear a few BIRDS starting up their songs.*)

LOIS. There, you see? The birds are real.

EARL. They're probably on salary.

LOIS. Wouldn't it be nice if we could spend another day here?

EARL. Nah, it's starting to depress me.

LOIS. Aw, c'mon. Look how beautiful the Matterhorn is in this light. I bet they designed it special so it would catch the sunrise on its peaks.

EARL. It wasn't designed for the sunrise. No one sees it in the sunrise.

LOIS. So? Maybe they did it for the milk men of Orange County.

EARL. It's not like it's a natural phenomenon. It's a fucking hunk of cement. They paint it white, we're supposed to believe it's snow.

LOIS. C'mon, let's try and enjoy our last moments here, O.K.?

EARL. Yeah.

LOIS. You thinking happy thoughts?

(EARL doesn't say anything.)

LOIS. You thinking about what we just did up in the tree? *(A beat.)* What are you thinking?

EARL. I'm thinking that tomorrow, we have to show up for Welfare.

LOIS. We better go get Chrissie.

(EARL takes LOIS' hand and leads her down.)

EARL. The leaves on this tree. They're made of vinyl. You notice that?

LOIS. Yeah, Earl. Yeah.

FADE OUT

Scene 9

In front of the restaurant in The New Orleans section. EARL is carrying CHRISSIE who is wrapped up in some blankets and still groggy. LOIS is carrying all their bags.
The dawn has turned the LIGHT pink.

LOIS. How do you think we should leave?

EARL. They got the gates locked. We're gonna have to wait 'til they open.

LOIS. Maybe we should hide in a rest room 'til then.

EARL. I don't want to spend my last hours here holed up in some stinking bathroom. We'll get in the canoe, go back to the Island.

CHRISSIE. I'm hungry.

LOIS. I know, sweetie. We're gonna go to the Food Bank later and get you something to eat.

CHRISSIE. My stomach hurts.

LOIS. Chrissie, you want to see something pretty? Look at the Matterhorn with all the pink. Look how it reflects in the lagoon. Isn't that beautiful?

CHRISSIE. (*Whimpering.*) Yes...

EARL. (*Goes to a trash can.*) Maybe someone left a box of popcorn or something.

LOIS. No, not from the trash.

EARL. We aren't gonna get to the food bank for hours. And then what if we get stuck in traffic and everything gets handed out before we get there?

LOIS. She could get a disease from the trash.

EARL. I'm not gonna give her something dirty. There are isolated parts that are clean.

LOIS. Maybe if one of the guards finds us they'll give us something for Chrissie to eat.

EARL. The guards aren't gonna care. They're gonna tell us to get the hell out.

CHRISSIE. Mommy, my stomach hurts.

LOIS. I know. Let's see if I have anything in my purse. You want to / help me look?

EARL. (*Looking through the trash can.*) Jesus, they cleared everything away already.

LOIS. Let's read our tickets and see what they say. / Do you know what that word is?

EARL. What the fuck is the matter with this place? (*Kicks the can several times.*)

LOIS. Earl, stop it. Come on, calm down will you? (*To Chrissie.*) Do you know what this word is?

CHRISSIE. Uh-uh. Mommy, my stomach hurts.

EARL. I'm gonna go find her some food.

LOIS. Where? There's nothing to find here.

(EARL exits.)

LOIS. Chrissie, can you tell me what this word is? "Welcome." See how it's spelled?

(EARL comes back in dragging an ice cream cart. The cover is bolted.)

EARL. Look what I found.

LOIS. Earl, it's locked.

(EARL frantically searches for some kind of tool.)

LOIS. What are you doing?

EARL. I'm looking for something to break it open with.

LOIS. You want to get yourself arrested?

EARL. What, for trying to feed my kid? *(EARL pulls out his keys and tries to unscrew one of the hinges with the tip of a key.)*

LOIS. *(To Chrissie.)* Can you tell me this word? "Magic." See? That's an M, that's an A, that's a G ...

(EARL stuffs the keys back in his pocket and runs off.)

LOIS. Earl? Where are you going? *(To Chrissie.)* Do you know what this word is? "Kingdom." Can you read this whole sentence now?

(CHRISSIE shakes her head.)

LOIS. "Welcome to the Magic Kingdom" See?

CHRISSIE. *(Crying.)* I'm hungry.

LOIS. Here honey, here's some Chapstick. Put it on your lips. It's flavored.

(EARL comes back in with a brick. HE starts banging the cart.)

LOIS. Jesus, Earl, come on. We're guests here. Don't go around wrecking things.

CHRISSIE. Is Daddy trying to get food?

LOIS. No, honey. He can't.

EARL. Don't tell her that. Don't tell her I can't do something.

LOIS. That's not what I'm doing.

EARL. I'm trying to help her.

LOIS. Earl, come on, you're destroying the property.

EARL. Fuck the property. Our kid is starving. This is America. This shouldn't be fucking happening in the first place.

LOIS. Earl, please. I'm hanging on by a thread here. Don't go crazy on me.

EARL. I'm trying to look for solutions here and everything I try to do, you're cutting me off.

LOIS. I'm not trying to cut you / off.

EARL. You are. You're cutting me off at / the balls.

LOIS. I'm trying to conserve our energy so when it comes time to do something we'll have the energy with which to do.

(CHRISSIE is starting to eat the Chapstick.)

LOIS. Chrissie, no. / Don't eat that.

EARL. Chrissie, what are you doing? Christ, our kid is eating Chapstick. *(EARL picks up the garbage can and starts smashing it against the ice cream cart.)*

LOIS. Earl, Jesus! What are you doing?

(LOIS gets up to stop him, still yelling. EARL continues to bludgeon the cart.)

LOIS. Earl, *stop!*

EARL. Shut up!

(CHRISSIE picks up the brick that Earl dropped and goes to help.)

LOIS. Chrissie, get back. Come on, Earl, stop! *(LOIS pulls on Earl's arms trying to stop him.)*
EARL. Get the fuck away from me! *(EARL shoves Lois to the ground.)*

(The top of the cart begins to give way. EARL is down on his knees, starting to pry it open. CHRISSIE runs up behind Earl. As EARL rips the lid open, his elbow hits Chrissie in the face.
LOIS screams and CHRISSIE starts to cry. The cart falls opens. It's empty except for a few napkins that spill out.)

LOIS. My God, Earl. My God, look what you've done.
EARL. Chrissie? Chrissie? Oh, Jesus.

(LOIS bends over Chrissie.)

EARL. I'm an asshole. I'm such an asshole.
LOIS. Chrissie. Chrissie honey, are you all right?
EARL. Chrissie, Daddy's sorry. He didn't / mean to hurt you.
LOIS. Earl, what did you do?
EARL. Chrissie, I'm so sorry. Daddy didn't mean to do that. He's so sorry. You forgive me Chrissie?
CHRISSIE. Did you get the ice cream?
EARL. No, baby.

LOIS. She has a bump.

EARL. Chrissie, you forgive me?

LOIS. That was a foolish thing you did.

EARL. I know.

LOIS. We aren't gonna get out of here unnoticed. They're gonna be going over the whole park looking for whoever did this.

EARL. I know.

LOIS. Maybe when the guards come, we can explain to them.

EARL. Explain what? There's no explaining.

LOIS. If I talk to them, if I explain about Chrissie.

EARL. Lois, they're gonna take one look at Chrissie, they're gonna take her away from us.

LOIS. No they won't.

EARL. They're gonna see the bruise on her head, they're gonna look at us looking like bums, they'll take her away.

LOIS. They wouldn't do that.

EARL. They do it all the time. We've seen it.

(A beat.)

LOIS. Oh Earl, I don't know what to do.

EARL. Listen to me.

LOIS. I don't know how this happened. How did we get to this?

EARL. Lois, listen. You and Chrissie hide in the rest room. I'll stay here, tell them I did it. Then when the park opens, you get in the car, you drive away.

(EARL digs in his pocket and gives LOIS the car keys and the rest of their money.)

LOIS. Early, no. Hide with us.

EARL. Go on.

LOIS. Early, I don't want to be without you.

EARL. We can't be together. I fucked up.

LOIS. No you didn't.

EARL. Lois, let me explain to you. Last night, it will never be that good again. You understand? I'm only gonna start being shittier to you. You aren't gonna want me around.

LOIS. Things will get better.

EARL. I hit you.

LOIS. You shoved me, you were upset, you only shoved me.

EARL. I was trying to hit you.

LOIS. You can't leave us, how am I gonna keep track of you?

EARL. I'll write to you.

LOIS. Where?

EARL. That postal box we rented to get the money for the lottery ticket? I'll write to you there. You remember the place?

LOIS. I don't know what I'll do without you.

EARL. You'll do OK. *(Hugging Chrissie.)* Daddy loves you, Chrissie. He loves you very much. *(To Lois.)* O.K. you better get out of here.

LOIS. No, Earl.

EARL. Go.

LOIS. I don't want to leave you.

EARL. I'll write to you. When they let me out, / I'll write.

LOIS. I'll come and get you. As soon as you get out, let me know where you are.

EARL. I will. Go on.

LOIS. I love you very much, Earl. You remember that.

EARL. I love you too.

*(LOIS takes CHRISSIE by the hand and walks off.
CROSS FADE to EARL and the COP. The COP offers him a cigarette. THEY both light up.)*

EARL. When we drove out here, we spent the nights parked at rest stops along the highways. I would like to compliment the park service for having such nice facilities that are actually open to the public. So at one of the rest stops, my wife comes out of the bathroom, she tells me she saw a note taped up on one of the mirrors. The note said: "I'm trying to get to Oregon and my car broke down. I need something to eat for my kids. I'm in the blue Chrysler out front." So we look outside the bathroom and there's this beat-up Chrysler parked next to one of those giant vacation trailers. And we see the woman sitting in the front seat with the doors locked and all the windows rolled up and a bunch of wound-up kids wrestling around in the back seat. And this retired couple from the trailer walks up to the car. And the old lady holds up a sandwich to the woman. And the woman rolls her window down just far enough to take the sandwich in, then she rolls it back up again, real quick. And my wife turns to me and says, "Isn't it terrible, Earl, that she doesn't have her husband with her and that she has to be so afraid." And I said, "If her husband

was with her, no one would want to help her and she
wouldn't be eating tonight."

(A beat.)

COP. So how did you end up this way?
EARL. I don't know. I lost my job and then... it was
like sitting in a bathtub full of nice hot water, watching it
go down the drain after someone's pulled the plug.

FADE OUT

END OF ACT I

ACT II

Scene 1

A welfare office. CHRISSIE is sitting in a dirty plastic chair looking through a magazine that looks like it's already been thumbed through by several hundred people. After a beat, LOIS joins her, holding a pile of welfare forms. SHE looks wrecked.

LOIS. Oh Chrissie, this is not a good day. Do you know what the lady's making me do? She's making me fill out the form all over again 'cause your legal name is Christine not Chrissie. Can you believe that?

CHRISSIE. (*Something in the magazine.*) Mommy what's this?

LOIS. It's someone's gum. Don't touch it. Just turn the page. (*Working on the form.*) It would of taken two seconds to change your name. I could've stayed there and changed it, we would've been out of here, but the stupid woman... / why do they do that, Chrissie?

CHRISSIE. (*Reading.*) That's a L... and that's a O... and that's a P...

LOIS. That's good, honey. You're doing your letters real good.

CHRISSIE. Shhh.

LOIS. What?

CHRISSIE. I'm talking to someone.

LOIS. Oh.

49

CHRISSIE. ...and that's a A and thaaaat's a N.

LOIS. Who are you talking to?

CHRISSIE. My friend.

LOIS. Oh, you have a new friend?

CHRISSIE. Uh-huh. I'm showing him how to read a magazine.

LOIS. That's good.

WOMEN'S VOICE. Number one-eighty-three. One-eighty-three. Ciento ochenta y tres. Ciento ochenta y tres.

LOIS. We're gonna be here all day. It's not like I filled the application out in / pencil for God's sake.

CHRISSIE. (*Re: magazine.*) That's a car and those are people in the car and they're going on a picnic. And they're going to eat chicken and carrot sticks and pie and vegetables and cookies / and they'll have things to drink...

LOIS. We aren't gonna make it to the food bank. If we get out of here in time, we'll go down to the shelter and have some dinner. Maybe that little girl will be there. Remember that little girl you talked to?

CHRISSIE. No.

LOIS. I think her name was Melanie. You liked her, Chrissie.

CHRISSIE. Do you know what that spells?

LOIS. What?

CHRISSIE. I'm talking to the angel.

LOIS. Oh.

CHRISSIE. (*Reading.*) "Honda."

LOIS. (*Looks down at the magazine.*) Chrissie, that's terrific. You read a word all by yourself. That's real good, honey.

CHRISSIE. The angel told me.

LOIS. Well the angel is very smart. Just like you.

CHRISSIE. (*Turns the page. Reading.*) "Royal Caribbean. When you're ready for something better."
LOIS. Chrissie? Did you read this?
CHRISSIE. It was told to me.
LOIS. Honey, did you maybe hear this on television?

(CHRISSIE shakes her head. SHE turns the page.)

LOIS. Maybe you did. Maybe you have a photographic memory. That's a good thing to have, a photographic memory.
WOMAN'S VOICE. One-eighty-four. One-eighty-four. Ciento ochenta y quatro. Ciento ochenta y quatro.
CHRISSIE. (*Reading effortlessly.*) "Take a ride in a Pontiac convertible and discover a whole new world of adventure. It's roomier, quieter and better performing."
LOIS. (*Looks down at the magazine. A beat.*) Chrissie…?

Scene 2

A mail box rental place in a crummy part of Hollywood. LOIS is talking to LAMAR standing behind the counter. CHRISSIE is restless. LOIS is strung out from welfare. LAMAR's answers should not appear stupid, just unyielding.

LOIS. I need to rent number one-fifty-three. You still have that box available?
LAMAR. Lemme check.

LOIS. Me and my husband rented it here last month. One-fifty-three.

LAMAR. I'm lookin'.

(CHRISSIE wanders over to the mail boxes and places her hands on them.)

LOIS. It was for a lottery ticket we won. That's the last time we rented it. We were just in here a couple of weeks ago, I don't know if you remember...

LAMAR. The box is taken.

CHRISSIE. Mommy?

LOIS. My husband is writing to me at that number.

LAMAR. You can't rent that box. You gotta rent another box.

CHRISSIE. Mommy?

LOIS. Chrissie, not now. *(To Lamar.)* If my husband sends me a letter to number one-fifty-three will you put it in the box I rent?

LAMAR. You can't rent one-fifty-three. It's taken.

LOIS. I know that.

CHRISSIE. Mommy?

LOIS. Chrissie, just wait a minute. *(To Lamar.)* What I'm asking is, if you get a letter addressed to me will you put it in the new box?

LAMAR. If it's got the number of the box you're renting.

LOIS. It's not gonna have that number. It's gonna be addressed to number one-fifty-three.

LAMAR. That box is taken, lady.

CHRISSIE. *(Over this, pointing to the boxes.)* Who's this? *(Giggles.)* Annnnd this? *(A beat.)* What's her name?

LOIS. (*Over this.*) I *know*. But the letter, it will have my name...

LAMAR. We don't go by names. We go by numbers.

LOIS. Then you'd put it in box number one-fifty-three?

LAMAR. That box is taken. Who's she talking to?

LOIS. She's just playing. Chrissie, come over here. (*Back to Lamar.*) What I'm asking is, if you get a letter and it says, "to so-and-so, box number one-fifty-three," you don't look at the name, you look at the number, right?

LAMAR. That's what I'm sayin'.

LOIS. O.K., so I'm asking, can we put a note in box one-fifty-three, explaining to the owner of that box that this one piece of mail is for me?

LAMAR. You gotta rent your own box. I don't give out no free mail.

LOIS. I said I'd rent another box. / I didn't say I wanted free mail.

LAMAR. There's only one individual per box. We don't allow no sharing / of the box.

LOIS. I said I'd rent another box.

LAMAR. Lotta people come in here they want two for one. We don't do that. You wanna rent your own box, that's fine. But don't come in here wanting / a free ride.

LOIS. That's not what I'm saying. I'm asking if whoever has the other box, if we can leave a note telling them / to return the letter to you.

LAMAR. You hafta rent a box before you get any mail.

LOIS. (*Very slowly.*) I said I'd rent a box.

LAMAR. You wanna rent a box, that's fine. But we don't give anyone free rides.

LOIS. Mister, I understand. But what I'm asking, is there some way you can take the letter that will be coming to me from my husband, is there some way to take that letter and put it in my *new* box with my *new* number instead of my old box which was one-fifty-three?

LAMAR. If your husband writes to you with the new number, we put it in the new box.

LOIS. He won't know the new number. He only knows the old number.

LAMAR. Then you tell him the new number.

LOIS. (*Loses it.*) Jesus Christ! You aren't listening to me! If I could tell my husband the new number I would have him write to me at the new number. Don't you think I'd do that? I know what I'm saying makes sense. Why are you treating me like I'm not making sense?!

(LAMAR just watches her.)

LOIS. I will say this one more time. I am *renting* a box. But I want to make sure that when my husband writes to me his letter will get to the box I *rent* and not to the *former* box. Is that possible? Is it possible for me to have his letter put in the new box? Or is this too complex for you to understand?

(A long beat.)

LAMAR. You ain't got any rights here. I hope you know that.

LOIS. Is what I asked, possible to do?

LAMAR. If you want his letter transferred you're gonna hafta pay a service charge.

LOIS. How much?

LAMAR. Two dollars.

LOIS. A month?
LAMAR. A day.
LOIS. What for?
LAMAR. Labor.
LOIS. For one letter?
LAMAR. I still gotta sort through the mail to see if it's there or not. That's a lotta labor.
LOIS. I can't afford it. I can barely afford the ten dollars for the box.
CHRISSIE. Mommy?
LOIS. What?
CHRISSIE. I can read the people's mail.
LOIS. Not now Chrissie. (*To Lamar.*) I can't give two more dollars. I need that money.
LAMAR. That's not my problem.
LOIS. This is for this little girl's father, for Christ sakes. This is the only way she'll be able to see him again. Look, I'll sort the mail myself. I'll come in here every day if I have to.

(*LAMAR stares off.*)

LOIS. You're a lousy person, you know that?
CHRISSIE. Mommy?
LOIS. What, Chrissie.
CHRISSIE. The angel and me have been looking at the mail in the boxes.
LOIS. Yeah.
CHRISSIE. (*Runs to one of the boxes and points.*) This is a welfare check... This is something from the army... This is something I'm not supposed to look at

'cause it's dirty... And this is a letter to a girl from her mother asking her to come home.

(*LAMAR stares at Chrissie.*)

LOIS. Oh yeah?
CHRISSIE. And the mother put yellow curtains up in her room and her cat had some kittens and Grandma Carey has been asking for her. And someone got a new pool.
LOIS. Chrissie, are you making this up?
CHRISSIE. No.
LAMAR. How you know number seventy-eight got somethin' dirty in't?

(*CHRISSIE just stares at Lamar.*)

LAMAR. How you know that, huh?
LOIS. Chrissie, what else do you know?
CHRISSIE. (*Walks over to another box and points.*) That one has drugs.
LAMAR. Shit, who is this kid?
LOIS. Come here, honey. Don't look at those anymore. (*To Lamar.*) I need to get my husband's letter. Are you gonna help me out here?
LAMAR. Yeah, O.K. I'll rent you a box. I won't charge you for the other thing. (*Throws a form and pencil on the counter.*) Fill that out.

(*As LOIS starts to write.*)

LAMAR. I'm doing you a favor. I hope you are aware of that.

FADE OUT

Scene 3

The children's section of a local library. CHRISSIE is reading a book at a table and LOIS is sitting beside her in a child size chair. SHE is watching Chrissie with almost a reverence.

CHRISSIE. (*Reading.*) "When Pinocchio awoke, he discovered that he was no longer a wooden puppet, but that he had become instead a boy. He gave a glance round and saw that he was in a pretty little room furnished and arranged with a simplicity that was almost elegance."
LIBRARIAN. (*Enters.*) We're closing now. I'm going to have to ask you to leave.
LOIS. All right. Thank you.

(The LIBRARIAN leaves.)

LOIS. (*To Chrissie.*) Honey, we have to stop now.
CHRISSIE. I want to hear the ending.
LOIS. I know. So do I.
CHRISSIE. Can we take the book?
LOIS. No, Chrissie, we can't get a card yet. We have to show them something that shows we have an address. Maybe I'll send a letter to our mail box, see if that works.
CHRISSIE. I want to read the book.
LOIS. We can come back tomorrow.
CHRISSIE. Can we take the book to the car?
LOIS. No.
CHRISSIE. Mommy, please?

LOIS. Chrissie, believe me, nothing would make me happier. I'd much rather be reading Pinocchio than staring at the dashboard all night.

CHRISSIE. The angel says it's all right to take the book.

LOIS. I don't think he did, Chrissie.

CHRISSIE. He said so, really.

LOIS. Chrissie.

CHRISSIE. He did, Mommy.

LOIS. Honey, don't use the angel as an excuse to do things you aren't supposed to do. That isn't nice.

CHRISSIE. I'm sorry. (*CHRISSIE hangs her head. And starts to cry.*) Mommy, I'm sorry. I didn't mean to.

LOIS. That's O.K., honey. It's O.K. Come on, let's go.

(LOIS takes CHRISSIE's hand and leads her off.
A beat.
The LIBRARIAN comes back in with a rag and some spray
    cleaner. SHE sprays the seats where Lois and Chrissie
    were sitting and starts wiping them off.)

FADE OUT

Scene 4

The car. It's night. CHRISSIE is in the back, hunched up
    in some blankets.
LOIS is in the front seat, trying to get a station on the
    radio. It's all STATIC. Finally SHE snaps it off.

LOIS. Someday, when Mommy and Daddy get a house again, we'll have a garden and we can grow our own tomatoes like Grandma used to do. You remember Grandma, Chrissie? Remember how she always cooked spaghetti?

(CHRISSIE doesn't respond.)

LOIS. And you'll have your own room. With carpeting and a pretty bedspread. And Daddy will build one of those desk units for you. That'd be nice. And you can pick any color to paint the walls. What color you want your room to be, Chrissie?

(CHRISSIE doesn't respond.)

LOIS. Chrissie? When you have your own room, what color would you like us to paint it?

(No response.)

LOIS. Honey, is the angel talking to you again?
CHRISSIE. Uh-huh.
LOIS. What is he saying?
CHRISSIE. He's playing music for me.
LOIS. What kind of music?
CHRISSIE. I can't explain it.
LOIS. Is it pretty?
CHRISSIE. Yes.
LOIS. That's good. I wish I could hear it. *(LOIS gets a baggy full of carrot sticks from the glove compartment and*

offers some to Chrissie to get her attention.) Chrissie tell me about your angel friend. Does he have a name?

CHRISSIE. Raphael.

LOIS. Oh. Is he Hispanic?

CHRISSIE. No.

LOIS. Where'd you get that name, Chrissie? Did you hear about him when we stayed at the mission?

CHRISSIE. No. I hate the mission.

LOIS. I know. Did you get this angel at Disneyland? Is he a friend of Tinkerbell's?

CHRISSIE. No.

LOIS. Can you see this angel?

CHRISSIE. Yes.

LOIS. What does he look like?

CHRISSIE. He's a man.

LOIS. What kind of man? Does he look like Daddy?

CHRISSIE. No.

LOIS. Does he look like Grandpa used to look?

CHRISSIE. No.

LOIS. Does he look like anyone you know?

CHRISSIE. No.

LOIS. What is he wearing? Is he wearing clothes?

CHRISSIE. Kind of.

LOIS. Are they robes?

CHRISSIE. I think so.

LOIS. Does he have wings?

CHRISSIE. He has something around his shoulders.

LOIS. What, like what?

CHRISSIE. A glowy thing.

LOIS. Like that picture you saw of Jesus in the mission?

CHRISSIE. No!

LOIS. It's a different glow?
CHRISSIE. Yes.
LOIS. And he talks to you?
CHRISSIE. Yes.
LOIS. What does his voice sound like?
CHRISSIE. His voice doesn't have a sound.
LOIS. Then how does he talk to you?
CHRISSIE. It's something in my head.
LOIS. Like a thought?
CHRISSIE. Yes.
LOIS. Did he tell you what was in the mail boxes?
CHRISSIE. Yes.
LOIS. Are you sure you weren't making it up?
CHRISSIE. Yes.
LOIS. Chrissie, you gotta tell Mommy if you're making this up. A lot of people are taking me around in circles and I gotta have someone around who isn't gonna do that to me. You understand?
CHRISSIE. Yes.
LOIS. So how did you know what was in the mail boxes?
CHRISSIE. The angel can see what everything is. Then he puts his head down next to mine and lets me hear.
LOIS. He touches his head to your head?
CHRISSIE. Uh-huh.
LOIS. What does it feel like?
CHRISSIE. Like air.
LOIS. Like a glow?
CHRISSIE. Yeah. And there's something here. (CHRISSIE touches her sternum.)
LOIS. He touches you there?
CHRISSIE. I feel something here.

LOIS. Like what?

CHRISSIE. The glowy thing.

LOIS. Is it in any other part of your body?

CHRISSIE. No.

LOIS. It's not down where you go to the bathroom? You don't feel anything there?

CHRISSIE. No.

LOIS. (*Touching her own sternum.*) It's only here.

CHRISSIE. Yes. (*Touching the side of her head.*) And here. When he talks to me.

LOIS. Oh, Chrissie. This is a very special thing. You have someone watching over you. (*LOIS hugs her.*) Do you think your angel can tell you where Daddy is?

CHRISSIE. I don't know.

LOIS. Well maybe you should ask your angel that.

CHRISSIE. Can I have another carrot stick?

LOIS. We have to save some for tomorrow.

CHRISSIE. I'm still hungry.

LOIS. I know, honey. You know what we're gonna do tomorrow? We're gonna go to a library and read some books. Would you like that?

CHRISSIE. I have to go to the bathroom.

LOIS. You have to make pee-pee?

CHRISSIE. Yes.

LOIS. O.K., hold on. Stay in, Chrissie, don't get out yet. (*LOIS unlocks her side and gets out of the car and looks around.*)

(*We hear a bottle CRASH and someone yell from somewhere, "FUCK YOU! I'M GONNA KILL YOU, GOD DAMMIT!"*)

LOIS. (*Getting back in.*) I don't like the looks of it here. Let me drive you to the gas station. You ask your angel something else, Chrissie. You ask him to find us a better place to park. (*As LOIS starts up the car:*)

FADE OUT

Scene 5

The mail box rental place. LOIS and CHRISSIE enter. LAMAR is sorting mail into the boxes. One of his hands is bandaged.

LOIS. Is that the mail for today?
LAMAR. Un-hunh.
LOIS. You know if I got anything?
LAMAR. I'll know when I'm done.
LOIS. I'm number two-eighty-one. Lois Randazzo.
LAMAR. Yeah, I know. (*LAMAR keeps sorting. He needs to get to a box where Chrissie is standing.*)
LOIS. Chrissie, move.
LAMAR. (*Holding up a letter.*) Hey, Chrissie, you know what's in this letter?

(*CHRISSIE shakes her head.*)

LAMAR. That's good. 'Cause you prob'ly don't wanna know. (*HE laughs.*)
LOIS. Chrissie, c'mere. You don't need to do that. (*To Lamar.*) Do you know how long this will take?

LAMAR. It will take me as long as it takes me.

LOIS. I know that. I just need to know how long we're going to be here for.

LAMAR. Lemme ask you something. You going anywhere? You got something important you gotta do? You got a job or somethin' you hafta go to?

LOIS. I can't get a job when I have a little girl to take care of. / That should be obvious. I'm tired of having to tell people this...

LAMAR. Excuse me, so you don't have a job? Is that correct?

(LOIS doesn't say anything.)

LAMAR. Fine. Then you can just si'down and wait. *(LAMAR goes back to sorting.)*

(LOIS sits with Chrissie. CHRISSIE is restless.)

LOIS. *(Trying to keep Chrissie occupied.)* We're getting our food stamps today. We'll go to the Ralph's, get us some good things to eat. You want to make a list with me? Let's make a list.

CHRISSIE. Mommy, you know the cat who had kittens? They gave all the kittens away except for one and they named it Mittens 'cause it has white on its feet.

LOIS. What cat are you talking about?

CHRISSIE. The girl's cat. Who the mother is writing to.

LOIS. The mother...

CHRISSIE. *(Pointing to the mail boxes.)* The *girl's* mother.

LOIS. Oh, right.

CHRISSIE. And Grandma Carey is sending her cookies.

LOIS. Uh-huh. (*A beat.*) What kind?

CHRISSIE. Toll House and Oatmeal.

LOIS. Oh. They sound good.

CHRISSIE. If the package is here, can we have one of the cookies?

LOIS. No, honey.

CHRISSIE. The angel said it's all right.

LOIS. Chrissie, what did I tell you about using the angel for the wrong thing?

LAMAR. I got a letter for you. Maybe it's your husband. Maybe he'll come and get you, take you off my hands. (*LAMAR hands the letter to LOIS. SHE immediately sees that it's her own handwriting.*)

CHRISSIE. Mommy, is that the letter we sent to us?

LOIS. No.

LAMAR. You sent a letter to yourself?

LOIS. It's to get a library card.

LAMAR. Un-hunh.

LOIS. That's right, mister. My daughter reads. Do you read?

LAMAR. Yeah, I read.

CHRISSIE. (*To Lois.*) Can I open it?

LOIS. (*Handing her the envelope.*) Don't wreck the envelope. That's the part we'll need. (*To Lamar.*) Chrissie is reading *The Hobbit* by J.R. Tolkien. You ever read anything by J.R. Tolkien?

LAMAR. I read other things.

LOIS. What?

LAMAR. Whatever needs to be read.

LOIS. Did you graduate high school?

LAMAR. Did you?

LOIS. Yes I did, as a matter of fact. I had a three point one grade average.

LAMAR. Is that right? Then how come I'm the one who's working and you're the one out on the street? Huh? How come you don't have that child in school? How come your hair is dirty? You better remember something when you come in here and talk to me, lady. I'm coming *out* of the shit, but you're the one who's going back into it.

(CHRISSIE touches Lamar's bandaged hand. HE startles.)

CHRISSIE. What happened to your hand?

LAMAR. I cut it. Had a accident.

(CHRISSIE keeps her hand on Lamar's.)

LAMAR. What're you doin'? You trying to heal me or somethin'?

LOIS. Chrissie, what are you doing?

CHRISSIE. I'm listening to his hand.

LAMAR. *(Pulling his hand away.)* You don't wanna do that. *(Goes back to sorting the mail.)*

CHRISSIE. *(To Lois.)* He makes pretty things with a air brush. *(To Lamar.)* What's a air brush?

LAMAR. Huh? *(Shyly.)* It's like a spray gun. For making fine art work on cars and things.

CHRISSIE. You once got mad at Rayline for touching it. Is she your little girl?

LAMAR. *(To Lois.)* This child don't have to be living offa welfare. She should be on a talk show or somethin'.

She could be making money. That's what I'd do if I were in your position.

CHRISSIE. The last time you saw your wife you gave her a key ring with Gemini the twins on it. You're supposed to send her money.

LAMAR. Uh-hunh.

LOIS. Oh, so you're one of those bastards who doesn't pay child support.

LAMAR. You wanna know what happens if I send my wife money? They take it outta her welfare check. That's right. There's no point in me givin' her all my money, having it taken away from her and then me ending up on welfare too. There's no point in that.

LOIS. Right.

LAMAR. Hey, don't you come in here passin' judgement on *my* head. You take care of your own damn business. Where's *your* husband? Where's *he* at?

LOIS. It's none of your business where my husband is.

LAMAR. Huh. I don't see no checks comin' in from him, do you? Hey Chrissie, put your hand on that box, see if there's any money in its future.

LOIS. You son of a bitch. This child loves her father. Don't start twisting up her mind. What's the matter with you?

LAMAR. (*Mumbling.*) Yeh, sorry.

LOIS. Bastard.

LAMAR. Yeh, OK, OK. It's the end of the month. You gonna renew your box?

LOIS. What's today?

LAMAR. The twenty-eighth. You got a problem with that?

LOIS. I just had a birthday. I forgot all about it.

LAMAR. Well, it happens.
LOIS. August twenty-sixth.
LAMAR. This is September. Shiiit, you don't even know what month you're in.

(LOIS takes CHRISSIE by the hand and starts to lead her out.)

LAMAR. Hey, wait a minute.

(HE takes an apple out of his lunch bag and tosses it to LOIS.)

LAMAR. Here. Happy birthday.
LOIS. Go to hell.

(SHE slams the apple back at him and exits with CHRISSIE.)

FADE OUT

Scene 6

The library. LOIS and CHRISSIE are standing in front of the librarian's desk. LOIS has a stack of books. The LIBRARIAN is examining an envelope.

LIBRARIAN. Is this your residence?
LOIS. That's our address.

LIBRARIAN. This is a postal box. Where is your residence?

LOIS. We don't use our regular address for our mail. We use the postal box. For dependability.

LIBRARIAN. Where is your residence?

LOIS. Delongpre Avenue.

LIBRARIAN. I'm going to need proof of that address.

LOIS. We don't get mail at that address.

LIBRARIAN. And the letter has to be from a bank, or a utility. We don't accept personal letters as a confirmation of address.

LOIS. These books are for my little girl to read. She loves to read.

LIBRARIAN. We'll be glad to give you a card if you can / give us proof of your address.

LOIS. Look, she's five years old and she's reading from *Charlotte's Web.*

(The LIBRARIAN is watching CHRISSIE.)

LOIS. Chrissie started to read on her own a couple of weeks ago. I taught her the alphabet and how to find letters but then she started to put it all together in her head. She did it without any help from me.

LIBRARIAN. Your child has head lice.

LOIS. Pardon me?

LIBRARIAN. Your child has head lice. I can't allow her in the reading room with the other children. I'm sorry. Please don't come back until you take care of this problem.

LOIS. Lady, what about this child's mind?

LIBRARIAN. I'm sorry to have to do this but I have to think about the other children who use this facility.

LOIS. She has a mind. She has a beautiful mind.
LIBRARIAN. I have to follow an ordinance. (*The LIBRARIAN takes the stack of books and leaves.*)
LOIS. This child is not a piece of garbage! Did you hear me? This child is not a piece of garbage!

(*LOIS sees that CHRISSIE is still holding* Charlotte's Web. *SHE takes it and puts it in her purse.*)

CHRISSIE. Mommy, you aren't supposed to do that.
LOIS. Never mind, let's go.

(*SHE grabs CHRISSIE's hand and leaves.*)

BLACKOUT

Scene 7

A park. LOIS is combing through CHRISSIE's head looking for vermin.

LOIS. I don't see anything Chrissie. I see some dandruff maybe, but I don't see any lice. And you know what? That was a run-around she was giving us about the address. We could of gotten a library card. That stupid woman didn't know what she was talking about.
CHRISSIE. She has an ovarian blockage.
LOIS. What?
CHRISSIE. That's what the angel said.

LOIS. Doesn't your angel have any useful information? We have seven dollars to last us for a week. Ask him why he didn't make sure the welfare didn't lose our check.

CHRISSIE. He can't do things like that. He can only watch.

LOIS. He can only watch, then how come he's helping you to read?

CHRISSIE. Because he likes to read.

LOIS. Then ask him why he doesn't talk to me. Ask him why he talks to you all night in the car and leaves me out.

CHRISSIE. The angel is looking at you, Mommy.

LOIS. Where? Show me where he is.

(CHRISSIE points.)

LOIS. There? By the tree? I don't see him. Is he saying anything to me?

CHRISSIE. No. He's just looking at you.

LOIS. It doesn't do me any good to have an angel looking at me if he isn't gonna help me out. Tell him I'm lonely. Tell him I need to have your daddy back. Tell him this is it. Tell that angel if he cares about you, to give us some help.

CHRISSIE. Mommy, he's waving at you. Mommy, look, he's waving.

LOIS. I'm glad to hear it, Chrissie.

BLACKOUT

Scene 8

A convenience store. LOIS is standing with CHRISSIE at the counter, talking to a CLERK.

LOIS. (*To Clerk.*) Do you have lottery tickets?
CLERK. How many you want?
LOIS. Could you do me a favor? Could you just show me a bunch of the tickets? I want to pick the one I'm gonna take. Is that O.K.?
CLERK. We don't do it that way.
LOIS. I'm not gonna touch any of them.
CLERK. How many you gonna buy?
LOIS. A couple. It depends.

(The CLERK reluctantly gets a sheet of lottery tickets and holds them up to Lois, keeping his distance.
LOIS hikes CHRISSIE up on the counter so she's face to face with the tickets.)

LOIS. Chrissie, take a look at these. Are any of them winners? (*A beat.*) Can you ask for help? (*A beat.*) Are you getting anything?

(CHRISSIE shakes her head.)

LOIS. (*To the Clerk.*) Can we see another one?

(The CLERK holds up another sheet.)

LOIS. (*To Chrissie.*) Even if it's just for ten dollars. That's all we need.

(A long beat. CHRISSIE is not responding.)

LOIS. Can we see another one, please?

(The CLERK holds up another sheet.)

LOIS. Chrissie, is there anything there or do you need to see some more?
CHRISSIE. I don't know.
LOIS. Honey, are you getting any help? Is he helping you at all? Close your eyes. Tell him what it's for. Tell him it's for the mail box. Tell him it's so you can see your daddy again. (*A beat.*) Chrissie, are you getting anything?
CLERK. You want a ticket or not?
LOIS. (*To Chrissie.*) You aren't getting anything?

(CHRISSIE shakes her head.)

LOIS. O.K., that's all right, honey.
CLERK. Are you gonna buy one?
LOIS. Yeah, I'll take one. (*LOIS hands him a dollar and the clerk tears off a ticket for her. LOIS lays the ticket down on the counter and scratches it with her nail.*) Hey, look at that. I won two dollars.
CLERK. You wanna cash it in or get two more tickets?
CHRISSIE. (*Points to some tickets.*) I want that one and that one.
LOIS. You think we should take those? You have a feeling about them?
CHRISSIE. Yes.

LOIS. Yeah, we'll take those.

(The CLERK tears the tickets for Lois.)

CHRISSIE. Can I scratch them, Mommy?
LOIS. Sure, honey. You know how to do it? Here, let me give you a penny. (*LOIS digs in her purse. Handing CHRISSIE the penny.*) Here. Scratch it with this.

(CHRISSIE scratches the ticket.)

LOIS. This part. Scratch it up here. (*LOIS watches as the numbers appear.*) Ten... fifty... ten... ten... Chrissie we got three tens! Honey look! We won ten dollars. (*SHE hugs Chrissie.*) Here, do the other one.

(CHRISSIE starts wildly scratching the next ticket.)

LOIS. (*To the Clerk.*) I told you I had a method. You watch, this is gonna be a big winner.
CHRISSIE. Mommy?
LOIS. What do we have here, Chrissie? (*LOIS looks then screams.*) A hundred dollars! We got a hundred dollars! Oh, Chrissie! (*LOIS hugs Chrissie.*)
CLERK. (*To Chrissie.*) Hey, you wanna pick one out for me?
LOIS. Chrissie, Chrissie, it's a miracle! You did a miracle!
CLERK. Lemme see 'em. (*The CLERK takes the tickets.*)

LOIS. I'm gonna buy us dinner, Chrissie. We're gonna have a big dinner to celebrate. / I wish Daddy could see this, he'd be so proud.

CLERK. Lady, hey lady.

LOIS. Go pick out something for yourself. / You deserve a treat.

CLERK. Lady, your kid scratched into the serial number.

LOIS. What?

CLERK. Your kid scratched into the serial number. You can't turn these tickets in.

LOIS. What do you mean?

CLERK. There's a number down here. It's a code thing. You scratch into it, the ticket's no good.

LOIS. These aren't any good?

CLERK. No, they're wrecked. You should never let a kid do a lottery ticket. They always mess it up.

(LOIS stares at the tickets.)

CHRISSIE. Mommy, I'm sorry. I didn't mean to do it.

LOIS. It's not your fault, Chrissie.

CLERK. You wanna try it again?

LOIS. Chrissie, you think you could pick another ticket out?

(CHRISSIE stares at the tickets then points.)

CLERK. This one?

(CHRISSIE nods.)

CLERK. (*Before he gives the ticket to Lois.*) It's a dollar.

(*LOIS digs a dollar out of her wallet. SHE takes the ticket and scratches it with Chrissie's penny.*)

CLERK. Anything?
LOIS. Chrissie, did the angel tell you to pick this ticket?

(*CHRISSIE doesn't say anything.*)

LOIS. Did he or didn't he? Shit, Chrissie. I wasted a dollar.
CHRISSIE. I'm sorry, Mommy. I didn't mean to.
LOIS. Just think next time, will you?
CHRISSIE. (*Crying.*) I'm sorry.
LOIS. Chrissie, that was our last dollar.
CLERK. Hey, don't pick on the kid.
LOIS. I'm not picking on her.
CLERK You're messing with her head.
LOIS. You talk to the Welfare about messing with her head. You talk to them about losing our food stamps in the computer and it'll be a "week to ten days" before we eat again.
CLERK. O.K., I'm just telling you to go easy on the kid...
LOIS. Hey. If you care about this child, then you give her something to eat. You have a store full of food and you can't pack something in a bag to give this child some lunch? Is that gonna put you out of business?

(A beat. The CLERK takes a bag and throws in a couple of apples and some sticks of beef jerky. HE hands it to Lois.)

CLERK. Here.
LOIS. *(Too humiliated to take it.)* Chrissie, go ahead.
CHRISSIE. *(Takes the bag. In a little voice.)* Thank you.

(LOIS starts to lead her out.)

CLERK. *(To Lois.)* Hey, you're welcome.

BLACKOUT

Scene 9

The mail box place. LAMAR is present. LOIS and CHRISSIE come trudging in. LOIS heads for the mail box.

LOIS. *(To Lamar.)* I don't have anything in the meter. Tell me if if you see the son-of-a-bitch parking people come by.
LAMAR. Un-hunh.

(CHRISSIE is clutching a book to her chest.)

LAMAR. *(To Chrissie.)* What you got there?
CHRISSIE. A book.

LAMAR. Un-hunh. What's it called?
CHRISSIE. *Charlotte's Web.*
LAMAR. Un-hunh. What's it about?
CHRISSIE. A spider who saves a pig.
LAMAR. Yeah? And how does a spider go about saving a pig?
LOIS. We got a letter. Chrissie, look we got something. Oh, Chrissie. I think it's from Daddy.

(CHRISSIE joins her. LOIS opens the envelope and pulls out the letter.)

CHRISSIE. (*Tries to grab it.*) Can I read it?
LOIS. Wait a minute, honey.
CHRISSIE. (*Reading.*) "Dear Lois..."
LOIS. Wait a minute, Chrissie, let Mommy read it. (*Reading.*) "Dear Lois, I hope you get this letter. I couldn't remember the number of the box we had so I'm taking a chance and just writing to the address."
LAMAR. There wasn't no number on the letter but I put it in your box anyway. I did that for you.
LOIS. Uh-huh. (*Continuing letter.*) "I was held over night at the Orange County Jail and the next day they let me go because Disneyland decided to drop the charges probably because they didn't want to hassle with the publicity. I've been traveling around since then and found some work in Covina digging holes for power poles. (*LOIS checks the envelope for money. Nothing.*) "I then met a guy who showed me how to jump trains and I've been doing some extensive traveling. I'm sorry I didn't write sooner. I just thought it'd be better for all of us if we spent some time apart for while. But I think about you and

Chrissie all the time and I miss you a lot. I'm going to write you again and maybe by then I'll have a mail box where you could write to me. Give Chrissie a hug for me and tell her that Daddy loves her very much. And I love you too. Love, Earl."

CHRISSIE. Are we gonna see Daddy?

LOIS. Not for a while, honey.

CHRISSIE. Where did he go?

LOIS. (*Looks at the post mark on the envelope.*) Oregon.

CHRISSIE. Where's that?

LOIS. Above California. (*To Lamar.*) Why did he wait three months to tell me this? What was I doing giving up a meal a week so I could pay for the God damn postal box? What if I gave up after a month and his letter never got to me? He would of never seen us again. What was he thinking?

LAMAR. Men, they're bad.

LOIS. He's expecting me to put out ten dollars a month, keeping up my end, making sure our little girl doesn't starve to death and he's off in Oregon doing "extensive traveling." What the hell is that?

LAMAR. Yeah, I wouldn't put up with that shit if I was you. Chrissie, c'mere, you want half 'o my sandwich? Here, I'm gonna wrap it up for you. You can take it for later. (*To Lois.*) Yeah, your husband, he's exhibiting some very bad behavior. (*LAMAR wraps the sandwich.*) It's the end of the month. You gonna renew your box?

(*LOIS doesn't say anything.*)

LAMAR. I'll give you a special rate. Five dollars.

LOIS. No. The hell with him. But thank you for the offer.

LAMAR. Tell you what, I won't rent it to no one else. In case you change your mind.

LOIS. All right.

CHRISSIE. Mommy?

LOIS. What, honey.

CHRISSIE. (*Pointing to a mail box.*) Grandma Carey died. She's with the angels.

LOIS. Good for Grandma Carey. (*To Lamar.*) You know all this time, I don't know what your name is.

LAMAR. Lamar.

LOIS. O.K., Lamar. (*To Chrissie.*) Come on, sweetie. We're gonna go yell at the welfare.

FADE OUT

Scene 10

The library. LOIS and CHRISSIE enter. The LIBRARIAN is at the desk.

LOIS. Excuse me.

LIBRARIAN. Yes?

LOIS. I would like to apply for a library card.

LIBRARIAN. Now look...

LOIS. Here is my proof of address. (*LOIS hands the librarian an envelope.*)

LIBRARIAN. This is from the welfare department.

LOIS. That's right.

LIBRARIAN. We require a utility bill.

LOIS. I don't use the utilities because my daughter and I live in a car. Do you have a problem with that?

LIBRARIAN. I'm sorry but I'm going to need more than a letter from the / Welfare Bureau...

LOIS. Wait a minute, do you have a problem with the fact that I have no where to live right now? Do you think that's a reason not to give my little girl the right to check out your books?

LIBRARIAN. I can't give you a card without the proper / verification...

LOIS. Answer me yes or no. Do you think that someone who doesn't have anywhere to take a shower doesn't have the right to read? Do you think that?

LIBRARIAN. No.

LOIS. I'm glad you don't. Because lady, if you lost your home, I promise you, you'd smell just as bad as I do. Let me tell you something. I used to have a house with my husband and he had a job. And yes, we used the utilities and every month we'd pay the bill. And I'd get calls on the phone and letters in the mail. And every day I had people to talk to who liked me. And one thing, just one thing had to go wrong to take that away from me. There's a thin line. There's a very thin line that divides you from me.

(The LIBRARIAN doesn't say anything.)

LOIS. I'm not gonna steal your books, for God's sake, I'm just trying to keep my kid from turning into a vegetable.

(A beat. The LIBRARIAN hands Lois a form.)

LIBRARIAN. You can fill that out.
LOIS. Go ahead, Chrissie. You can get your book.

(CHRISSIE runs off.)

LIBRARIAN You have to understand, there are people who come in here—there was a man who slept all day with his head on the table and lost control of his bladder in one of the chairs. I had a woman who came in to use the bathroom, she took off her clothes and was washing herself in the toilet. Little children use this library. It's hard enough for me to get them to come in at all.
LOIS. By the way, my child does not have head lice. She has been examined and she does not have head lice. You had no right to tell us that. *(LOIS fills out the card.)*
LIBRARIAN. *(Pulling out some change.)* I'd like you to have this.
LOIS. I wasn't asking you for money. I was asking for a library card.
CHRISSIE. *(Comes back with her book.)* Mommy, I found it.
LOIS. Give it to the lady. She'll check it out for you.

(CHRISSIE hands the librarian the book. The LIBRARIAN glances at her hands, checking for dirt. LOIS catches this.)

LOIS. Someone left a chocolate stain on page eighteen and there's a tear on page thirty-five. Perhaps you'd like to make a note of this.

LIBRARIAN. (*Embarrassed.*) That won't be necessary. (*The LIBRARIAN stamps the book and hands it back to Chrissie.*)
LOIS. (*Takes* Charlotte's Web *out of her purse and hands it to the Librarian.*) By the way, we enjoyed this very much.

FADE OUT

Scene 11

The car. It's night. CHRISSIE is in the front seat with LOIS, reading from Little House on the Prairie. *SHE's having a harder time with the words.*

CHRISSIE. "Then the sun went down far a-way in the w-est and it was t-ime to make the camp re-ady for night. Pa chained Pet and Pat-ty to the..." Mommy, what's that word?
LOIS. "Feedbox."
CHRISSIE. "...feedbox at the end of the..." (*CHRISSIE points.*)
LOIS. "...wagon. He chained Bunny to the side. And he fed them all their supper of corn."
CHRISSIE. Mommy, I don't hear the words anymore.
LOIS. Maybe you're just tired.

(*CHRISSIE looks up and stares at the air. SHE turns around, panicked, looks in the back seat.*)

LOIS. Chrissie, what? What is it?
CHRISSIE. I can't find him.
LOIS. The angel?
CHRISSIE. He's gone. Mommy, the angel is gone.
LOIS. Maybe he just stepped away.
CHRISSIE. Where did he go?
LOIS. Well, maybe he went to visit another little girl who needs him more. Or maybe he's hiding somewhere ...
CHRISSIE. I miss him.
LOIS. I know. (*A beat.*) Chrissie, you're gonna be a big sister in a couple of months. Can you believe it? Mommy didn't even know.
CHRISSIE. Know what?
LOIS. I'm gonna have a baby. Oh Jesus, Chrissie, I don't know how I'm gonna do this.

FADE OUT

Scene 12

THREE MONTHS LATER
The mail box place. It's night. The office section is closed. LOIS and CHRISSIE enter. LOIS is now noticeably pregnant. SHE keeps Chrissie close to her, aware that they're alone in a bad neighborhood. THEY go to their box.

LOIS. (*Opening the box.*) Ooh, Chrissie, look. You got some mail. It's that thing we sent for from the cereal box.

(*SHE hands a small package to Chrissie.*)

LOIS. (*Pointing to the label.*) See what that says?
CHRISSIE. (*Reading.*) "Mrs. Chrissie Randazzo."
LOIS. "Ms." That says "Ms. Chrissie Randazzo."

(*CHRISSIE starts tearing open the box.*)

LOIS. Honey, don't open it here. Save it for the car.

(*There's a MAN lurking outside. We can only see a shadow, a glimpse of a coat.*)

CHRISSIE. I wanna open it.
LOIS. Chrissie not now... (*LOIS stares at the open door. SHE's aware that someone's out there.*) Let's just wait here for a second until that man goes away.

(*LOIS waits. The MAN doesn't move.*)

LOIS. Shit. Honey, get behind me. Stay behind me. (*LOIS grabs one of the plastic chairs and holds it in front of her like a weapon.*)

(*The MAN moves into the doorway.*)

LOIS. (*Screaming like a mad woman.*) GET AWAY! GET AWAY FROM HERE OR I'LL KILL YOU!

EARL. Lois! Lois, it's Earl!

LOIS. Oh, Jesus!

EARL. It's me. I didn't / mean to scare you.

LOIS. Earl! My God where did you come from?

EARL. I went down the street for a soda, I was just coming back, / I was waiting for you.

LOIS. Oh my God, my God...

EARL. I was sitting here waiting for you all day. I just stepped out. I didn't mean to scare you.

LOIS. Well yeah, yeah you did. My God.

EARL. (*Puts a knapsack down that he's been carrying. HE looks healthier, his skin is tan, like he's been spending a lot of time outdoors.*) You remember your Daddy, Chrissie?

(CHRISSIE runs to Earl.)

EARL. Yeah, she remembers me. My little girl remembers me. (*Turning back to Lois.*) Hello, Lois.

LOIS. So you've come back?

EARL. Yeah, I've come back.

LOIS. Just like that, you're here?

EARL. Yeah, I'm here. (*A beat.*) So how long you been pregnant?

LOIS. Jesus, what do you think? Count back.

EARL. You been eating? You been taking care of yourself?

LOIS. Yeah, I've been taking care of myself.

EARL. I went to the grocery, bought you some food. Got some of those juices in the boxes you like, some bread, some peanut butter. Some nice apples.

LOIS. So you're providing for us now?

EARL. I got here at eight in the morning to wait for you. I've been here all day, talked to the guy who works here. He told me everything that's been happening with you. He said you're doing OK.

LOIS. Uh-huh.

EARL. Chrissie, I got you a treat.

(EARL gives Chrissie a candy bar.)

EARL. *(To Lois.)* I've been making some money. I want to take you and Chrissie out to dinner. We'll go to one of those places you like, with the salad bar. Chrissie, you wanna do that, have a nice dinner with Daddy?

CHRISSIE. Yeah! *(Pointing to label.)* Daddy, look. I can read this. "Snickers."

EARL. Hey, that's really good. *(To Lois.)* She starting to read now?

LOIS. Yeah, she reads.

CHRISSIE. I read a whole book.

EARL. She's reading books?

LOIS. Yeah, a few.

CHRISSIE. An angel taught me.

EARL. Oh yeah? *(To Lois.)* What was this?

LOIS. Nothing.

EARL. We should find a place to put her in school.

LOIS. I've taken care of that.

EARL. Chrissie, I got something else for you. *(HE hands Chrissie a shell.)* I found this on a special beach. Hold it up to your ear. You can hear the ocean.

LOIS. So what, you're asking to come back? After I've done all the work, you're asking to be a part of the family again?

EARL. (*Gets out his wallet and pulls out a wad of bills.*) All of the money I made, I'm handing it over to you.

(*LOIS won't take the money.*)

EARL. This is yours. This is for you and Chrissie.
CHRISSIE. Daddy, can I hold it?
EARL. You can hold a little bit of it. (*Hands her a dollar.*)
LOIS. What, you're providing for us so now you can leave?
EARL. No, I'm showing you I don't consider this my money. I made this money to give to you. I'm putting you in charge of it. I'm not leaving you again, Lois.
LOIS. Yeah, well that's still under discussion.
EARL. You're gonna have this baby alone? You're gonna do it without me?

(*LOIS doesn't say anything.*)

EARL. I have a job. I'm gonna take care of you.
LOIS. I have my own job.
EARL. Yeah? That's wonderful. Where're you working?
LOIS. At an elementary school. I'm a cross walk guard. They're also considering me for a bus driver position.
EARL. That's terrific. I just got a job in a tire shop. I guess we both have jobs that are traffic related. (*A beat.*) So is the car holding up? Is it running OK?
LOIS. Something's wrong with the heater. It blows from only one vent and it makes a terrible smell.
EARL. Maybe something crawled up there.

LOIS. That's what I figure.

EARL. Want me to look at it?

LOIS. Yeah, well the bastards at the gas station won't help me.

EARL. After I take you to dinner I'll take a look at it.

LOIS. I don't know if we're going to dinner with you.

CHRISSIE. Mommy, please? I want to have dinner with Daddy.

EARL. She been getting enough to eat?

LOIS. You dare to ask me that question? After leaving us alone for six months you dare to be asking about your daughter's well-being?

EARL. You have every right to be pissed at me.

LOIS. I know that already.

EARL. I'm sorry. That's all I can say, I'm truly sorry it had / to be this way.

LOIS. You can't just show up after six months and make nice with us. It's not gonna work that way.

EARL. I know, I know that...

LOIS. For six months, Earl, six months I've been hanging on. How'd you know I'd be able to keep up payments for a postal box that long? How'd you know I'd even want to bother with you anymore?

EARL. I was going on faith, Lois.

LOIS. Fuck faith! Fuck your faith! You left us alone out here with no protection! What do you think it's like to sleep in a car with a terrible stink with all the windows rolled up because you're afraid some man is gonna reach in and try to hurt you?!

EARL. Baby, I know.

LOIS. No you don't! We almost starved, did you know that? The welfare lost our check, they almost let us *starve,* for God's sake! God damn it, Earl, I'm carrying your child! It's a wonder it's still alive! How could you get me pregnant and then disappear! / How could you do that?!

EARL. I came back, I was never gonna not come back...

LOIS. How could I know that! You left us out here! We could of disappeared! We could of been killed!! You could have lost us!

EARL. Lois ... (*Tries to put his arm around her.*)

LOIS. THE HELL WITH YOU! GO AWAY AND LEAVE US ALONE!! GO AWAY!! (*LOIS beats at Earl with her fists.*)

CHRISSIE. Mommy stop it! Stop hitting Daddy!

(*LOIS finally stops. EARL is holding his nose. CHRISSIE is crying.*)

LOIS. Did I hurt you?

(*EARL takes his hand down. There's blood on his nose.*)

LOIS. Oh, shit, Earl.

EARL. I'm OK. I'll be OK.

LOIS. You want me to drive you to the hospital?

EARL. Naa, it's a surface thing. It's OK.

LOIS. It's OK, Chrissie, Daddy's all right. Nothing happened. He's all right. (*Crying.*) Oh, dammit, Earl.

EARL. There's a Sizzler over on Sunset, we can go sit. I'll buy you some dinner. After we eat I'll go away if you want. I'll leave you alone. (*A beat.*) You wanna do that?

(LOIS nods.)

EARL. Want me to drive?

(LOIS hands him the keys.)

CHRISSIE. Daddy, can I go to the salad bar?
EARL. As many times as you want. You gotta pace yourself, though.
CHRISSIE. I know. And I'm gonna have vegetables. And something hot.
EARL. That sounds good.
CHRISSIE. Then will you take us home?
EARL. I can't do that for you right now, Chrissie.

(EARL holds the door open for Lois. SHE exits and HE and CHRISSIE follow.)

FADE OUT

Scene 13

The car. It's after dinner. EARL is taking apart the heater. LOIS and CHRISSIE are keeping a distance.

LOIS. Oh, Jesus, what is it? Is it a rat?
EARL. It's a lizard.
CHRISSIE. Let me see.
EARL. No, you don't wanna look at it.

LOIS. I thought it was a giant rat, the way it's been stinkin' up the car.

CHRISSIE. Daddy, we used your after-shave to keep the smell away.

EARL. Yeah?

LOIS. Yeah, well I found the bottle under the seat.

EARL. Did it work?

LOIS. It was better than a rotting animal smell, yeah. (*To Chrissie.*) Chrissie, it's time for you to go to bed.

CHRISSIE. I want to stay up with Daddy.

LOIS. I want you to go to sleep. You have a big day tomorrow.

CHRISSIE. Nooo, I want to see Daddy.

EARL. You want me to tell you a bedtime story, Chrissie? I'll tell you about the beach I went to with the whales.

CHRISSIE. Yeah!

LOIS. Chrissie, get in the car. Put your jammies on. I'll be there in a minute.

(*CHRISSIE whines.*)

LOIS. *Now,* Chrissie. (*LOIS leads CHRISSIE to the car and shuts the door. Turning on Earl.*) You haven't told me shit where you've been all this time, and suddenly you want to tell our daughter bedtime stories?

EARL. Lois, what do you want me to do? You want me to say goodnight, never see / you again?

LOIS. That child makes her bedroom in the back seat of a car, she's scared to death to take a pee in the middle of the night, you want to tell her how Daddy's been lounging on a beach?

EARL. Jesus, no.

LOIS. Then what? What are you here for?

EARL. I'm here to help.

LOIS. After six months.

EARL. I was looking for a job so I'd have something to offer you. I wanted to come back at the right time so you wouldn't tell me to go to hell.

LOIS. But that's exactly what I'm doing.

EARL. So that's it? You never want to see me again? The marriage is over?

LOIS. You broke a trust.

EARL. I came back 'cause you and Chrissie are the most important thing in my life.

LOIS. You came back because it was convenient.

EARL. I let myself get arrested so you and Chrissie could escape.

LOIS. Oh fuck, Earl, so now you're a hero.

EARL. You aren't even giving me a chance.

LOIS. That's right.

EARL. If you think I'm such a piece of shit then you shouldn't of fucking married me in the first place. (*HE throws his wallet on the ground next to Lois and starts to walk off.*)

LOIS. Don't you throw your money at me!

EARL. Then don't you treat me like garbage! Don't you treat me like I'm not worth your fucking time!

(SOMEONE shouts from across the street: HEY, WHAT'S GOING ON OVER THERE?
There's a pause in the fight.)

CHRISSIE. (*Calling from car.*) Daddy?

EARL. Yeah, baby?

CHRISSIE. Are you still here?

EARL. Yeah, Chrissie, I'm right here.

CHRISSIE. Daddy c'mere.

LOIS. Chrissie, shut your eyes. I promise I'll let Daddy say goodnight to you before he goes.

(A beat.)

EARL. Did you tell her bad things about me?

LOIS. No. What would be the point?

EARL. I came so close to hurting her. I was mad at her for being hungry. I wanted to hit her.

LOIS. I wouldn't of let you. If you hurt Chrissie, I would of cancelled you from my life.

EARL. That's why I left. *(A beat.)* You still love me?

LOIS. What were you doing that was so important, you couldn't even write to me for three months?

EARL. I was in very bad shape.

LOIS. I'm sorry to hear that. I, on the other hand, was having a wonderful time.

EARL. Jesus, I know. I know it was hard for you. I'm sorry. I fell apart. I was doing bummy behavior and I didn't want you and Chrissie around me.

LOIS. Like what? Picking up hookers? Eating cats, what?

EARL. Would you let me tell you about the good things? The things I was doing that I wish you were there for?

LOIS. Yeah, go ahead.

EARL. I met a guy one night in a bar named Captain Jack. He talked me out of a fight, bought me some pretzels.

LOIS. Where was this?

EARL. Downtown.

LOIS. Downtown where? Here, downtown?

EARL. Yeah.

LOIS. You were here this whole time?

EARL. Some of the time, yeah.

LOIS. Oh, fuck, Earl.

EARL. Hey, since when did your language get so bad? You talk that way around Chrissie?

LOIS. That's not what we're discussing here.

EARL. You gonna let me go on?

(LOIS nods at him.)

EARL. So this Captain Jack took me down to the train yards. He showed me how to hop a train.

LOIS. Smart, Earl. You could of gotten yourself killed.

EARL. Nah, I was OK. We were on the Western Pacific heading up towards Oregon. After about a day of traveling we starting getting into the most beautiful scenery I'd ever seen. There were trees and mountains and the Feather River was right below us. And Jack was like this tour guide. He'd point at things and say, "That's the best place to catch trout," "That's a nesting ground for quail," "That's Dolly Parton Rock." And when we pulled into Oroville, we hopped off and he took me on a hike to this hobo camp. And the whole place is set up for your comfort. There were pots and plates and a beautiful fireplace all put together out of rocks. They even had a library set up with a bunch of old books. People borrowed on the honor system.

LOIS. You don't know what I had to go through to get a library card for Chrissie.

EARL. Yeah?

LOIS. They make it impossible.

EARL. Sure, of course. They always do.

LOIS. But I finally got her one.

EARL. You did? That's great. That's great, Lois.

LOIS. So go on. They had a library...

EARL. Yeah. So then Jack showed me this half a watermelon hanging from a tree. And I said, "What's that?" and he said, "We're makin' watermelon wine." See, you scoop out the pulp and you pack the watermelon with yeast and sugar and you let it set for a couple of weeks in the shade. He gave me some, it was fantastic, it was like this nectar of the Gods. And then he showed me how to dig for roots and find nuts and berries and he made us this dinner out of nature, this beautiful, delicious meal under this sky that was—there were no cities around, so it was very black with the stars very sharp and bright. And I kept telling myself, "I have to remember this to tell Lois. She would appreciate this. This would give her faith."

LOIS. Nice to know you were thinking of me.

EARL. I was, Lois. Oh, and you know what this guy said? He said when you're living on the outside of regular life you get down to the truth faster. He was living on less than we have and he was happy. He had dignity. The secret was, he wasn't ashamed of himself.

LOIS. He didn't have a little girl to take care of.

EARL. Yeah, so that's why I'm here.

LOIS. It's not settled yet.

EARL. Yeah, I know. I know that. (*A beat.*) Oh, you would of liked this. I ran into these two guys who hopped a train with me in Colton. Turns out they were living in Beverly Hills. One's a lawyer, the other a developer or something. They drive Mercedes, have pools, very wealthy guys. Once a year they put on old clothes and hop trains. This is like their vacation, right? They get off on being bums.

LOIS. They told you this?

EARL. No, this old 'bo told me. He's seen these guys all over the place. They think they're fooling everyone 'cause they've been wearing the same clothes for three days and they're a little ripe under the arms pits. But they have credit cards sewn into their jeans for when they get too dirty and they want to fly home.

LOIS. I believe it.

EARL. This one guy, we were sitting around the fire and he was cooking a potato on the end of a stick. I could tell he was getting off on the fact that this was the only thing he was gonna have for his dinner, right? He has this dreamy look in his eyes, like, "Isn't life just too good to be true." Then when the potato's done, instead of just biting into it like a truly hungry guy, he pulls out this brand new Swiss Army knife and starts cutting it into pieces.

LOIS. Unbelievable.

EARL. You shoulda seen their sleeping bags. These were these hundred percent goose-down numbers that must of cost five, six hundred dollars a piece. And they use these bags once a year.

LOIS. Well, there's an imbalance, Earl. There's a true imbalance.

(A beat.)

EARL. I'm gonna say goodnight to Chrissie. (*EARL opens the car door.*) Chrissie, you asleep?
CHRISSIE. No...
EARL. You wanna give me a kiss good night?
CHRISSIE. C'mere and sit with me.
EARL. (*Scoots in the back seat with Chrissie. HE sees something scotch taped to the back of the seat.*) Is this the birthday card I sent you?
CHRISSIE. Yeah.
EARL. Looks good there. (*Pointing to something else.*) And what's this?
CHRISSIE. That's a drawing I did of my friend.
EARL. Who's this friend?
CHRISSIE. Raphael.
LOIS. (*Throwing it away.*) She had a visitation, Earl.
EARL. Oh. Lois, why don't you come back here and sit with us?
LOIS. I think I'll stay out here for awhile.
EARL. Can I tell you another story?
LOIS. Go ahead.
EARL. About half-way up the coast there's this switch depot called Surf. The train slows down and you can hop off and you're right in the middle of a hundred miles of deserted beach. There's no trash. No people. It's a paradise. When I was there, I was hanging out with a couple of 'bo's. We were having a smoke and telling stories while we watched the sun set. And it was my turn to tell a story. I thought of telling them about all the shitty things that happened to us. But it was such a beautiful place, I just

didn't see the point. So I told them about our night in Disneyland. I told them everything, about sneaking on the island, watching the fireworks, going out in the canoe. They loved it. Especially the part when we broke the bed.

LOIS. You didn't!

EARL. Yeah. They raised their bottles in a toast to you.

LOIS. (*Laughing.*) They didn't.

EARL. "To lovely Lois." And about a month later when I was up in this camp in Oroville, someone started telling this story about the homeless couple who spent the night in Disneyland. And another guy said he knew that one already, he heard it in Montana. We're famous.

LOIS. Did you tell them who you were?

EARL. Yeah.

LOIS. What'd they say?

EARL. They gave me a road name. "Swiss Family Earl."

LOIS. Swiss Family Earl.

EARL. Come back and sit with us.

LOIS. (*Climbs into the back seat.*) I'm so tired, Earl. I need someone else to talk to. I've run out of stories to tell Chrissie. I've run out of decorating ideas for imaginary rooms.

(EARL puts his arm around Lois. SHE falls apart.)

LOIS. Oh Earl, you bastard, don't you ever leave me again. Don't ever do that to / me again.

EARL. I won't baby, I won't. I promise you with all my heart, I won't.

LOIS. Oh Early, I want to lay down on my own bed again. I want to sleep in a room where the floors are clean.

EARL. It'll happen baby, I promise. I promise, baby.

LOIS. Earl, did you know that the welfare owes us money? When we lost our place, they were supposed to give us emergency relief. We were entitled to be helped but they never told us that, Earl. I found a lawyer to help me. He'll work for free 'cause he likes to beat up on the / welfare.

EARL. Let me just hold you for a minute, Lois.

LOIS. Keep talking to me, please keep talking to me.

EARL. Before you have the baby, we can take a drive up to that special beach. I'll show Chrissie the dolphins and the whales jumping in the water. We're gonna spend all day at the beach and when the sun starts to set, we'll gather driftwood and make a fire and I'll cook you a delicious dinner. When it gets dark we'll all take a walk and I'll show you and Chrissie the constellations. Then we'll lay our blankets out on the sand and we'll fall asleep listening to the waves.

(Sound of OCEAN as we FADE OUT.)

END OF PLAY

COSTUME PLOT

LOIS
Pants
Shirt
Scarf
Sneakers
Shift
Sweater
Pregnancy pad

EARL
Jeans
T-shirt
Cap
Work boots
Jacket

CHRISSIE
Shorts
T-shirt
Pants
Sweater
Barrettes or hair ribbons
Sneakers
Pajamas

LAMAR
Stretch shirt
Pants
Expensive running shoes
Gold wrist chain

<u>COP</u>
Straw hat
Black poly pants
"1890's" shirt
Sleeve garter
Walkie-talkie

<u>CLERK</u>
Black t-shirt
Black pants
Walkman

<u>LIBRARIAN</u>
Suit—skirt and jacket
Silk or poly blouse
Heels

PROPERTY PLOT

Blankets
Purse and wallet for Lois
Hair grease for Lois and Chrissie (Act II)
Knapsack and wallet for Earl
Money
Rag doll for Chrissie
Hot dog
Ketchup bottle
Napkins
Lemon wedges
Plastic glasses
Plates
Salad
Rolls
Cigarette butt
Chapstick
Disneyland ticket
Ice cream cart with bolt
Brick
Car keys
Welfare form
Pen
Magazine
Letters
Charlotte's Web book
Carrot sticks in baggie
Pinocchio book
Spray cleaner and rag
Apple
California Lottery tickets

Coin
Candy bars
Little House on the Prairie book
Bag of groceries
Sea shell
Snickers bar

FURNITURE

Benches—can be doubled for other objects: canoe, sink,
    etc.
Chairs—can be doubled for other objects: car seats, etc.
Mail box unit
Counter—for mail room, library and convenience store